The Learning Layer

The Learning Layer

Building the Next Level of Intellect in Your Organization

Steven D. Flinn

THE LEARNING LAYER
Copyright © ManyWorlds, Inc., 2010.

Aspects of the descriptions in this book may be the subject of patents owned by ManyWorlds, Inc. This book does not constitute a license for, or an offer to license, ManyWorlds, Inc. patents, systems, or methods.

First published in 2010 by PALGRAVE MACMILLAN® in the United States - a division of St. Martin's Press LLC, 175 Fifth Avenue, New York, NY 10010.

Where this book is distributed in the UK, Europe and the rest of the World, this is by Palgrave Macmillan, a division of Macmillan Publishers Limited, registered in England, company number 785998, of Houndmills, Basingstoke, Hampshire RG21 6XS.

Palgrave Macmillan is the global academic imprint of the above companies and has companies and representatives throughout the world.

Palgrave® and Macmillan® are registered trademarks in the United States, the United Kingdom, Europe and other countries.

ISBN: 978–0–230–10301–6

Library of Congress Cataloging-in-Publication Data

Flinn, Steven D.
   The learning layer : Building the Next Level of Intellect
In Your Organization / Steven D. Flinn.
      p.   cm.
   Includes index.
   ISBN 978–0–230–10301–6
   1. Organizational learning.   2. Knowledge management.
   3. Information technology—Management.   I. Title.
   HD58.82.F59 2009
   658.3′124—dc22   2009049086

Design by Integra Software Services Pvt. Ltd

First edition: July 2010

10 9 8 7 6 5 4 3 2 1

Printed in the United States of America.

Contents

Part IV: Building Learning into the Fabric of *Your* Business

Preface

This book is a business manifesto clothed in technology trappings. I recognize that it has been a while since information technology (IT) has *truly* mattered to most business executives. Technology only really matters to businesses when it is capable of driving true competitive advantages. And for most of the past decade IT in the enterprise was basically on autopilot because there was nothing particularly transformational about it. Internet-based commerce and business reengineering were clearly transformational, but since then, not so much.

I'm going to make the case that it is time to pay attention again because the next wave of transformational IT has begun to take shape. You should know that I have a vested interest in this new wave—I founded a company that is actively working toward making these new capabilities a business reality. I've always oriented my professional life around trying to identify the inevitable, working backwards from that, and then acting accordingly. What I outline in this book I firmly believe is inevitable. And born of necessity, a requisite dose of naiveté, and I suppose a streak of stubbornness, I have personally acted to try to contribute to its inevitability by inventing and building a bit of the required foundations. The role that my company or any other company will ultimately play is uncertain, but the trend and the implications for your business are surely inevitable.

"The future has already arrived; it is just not evenly distributed yet." This is the famous quote attributed to science fiction writer William Gibson that launches a thousand technology presentations each year. It's a truism that implies that we just need to look hard enough and we will be able to see what will be important to us in the future. But here's the rub—the overwhelming majority of the obscure will not become an important part of our future, at least not in their present forms. So there are two ways to get things wrong about the future. For those of us with too much time on our hands, it is all too easy to get caught up in the moment and over-extrapolate from the vast number of current trends and then be surprised, and perhaps a bit disappointed, about the way the future actually unfolds. We take the noise to be the signal. On the other hand, the much greater number of us have too little time on our hands. Our intellectual spam filters are dialed to such a strong level that we are prone to not even glimpsing the important emerging trends until very late—and so the future sneaks up on us. In this book we are going to take an intellectual journey together leading to what I believe you will also conclude is an inevitable future. When the technically feasible begets the sublimely useful, there cannot be anything other than inevitability. We'll just let the future sneak up on the people who haven't read the book! And as we will see, this future very much starts now.

So what is the big, transformational, and inevitable idea? It is the idea that automatic *learning* capabilities will soon be embedded within the majority of business systems and processes. That these systems will routinely and automatically learn from the collective behaviors of the users of the system, and will reconfigure themselves accordingly. That these systems will automatically present themselves differently, for example, to novices than to experts. That these systems will generate recommendations of many varieties that will continuously guide their users. And that business processes will no longer be the brittle, one size fits all, monoliths that we are currently all too familiar with.

Smatterings of these *adaptive* capabilities have been increasingly presenting themselves on advanced Internet sites. But where I believe these capabilities can most effectively come together to amplify learning is in the *enterprise*. And that's the focus of this book.

The first two sections of the book are organized around the following simple but compelling path of logic:

1. Enhanced organizational learning drives *sustainable* competitive advantages for businesses.
2. The brain is a network that learns by *reconfiguring network connections* on the basis of experience.
3. IT systems can be structured as *reconfigurable networks* that adapt on the basis of the *collective behaviors* of the users of the systems. In other words, analogous to the brain, these systems can automatically *learn from experience*.
4. These adaptive IT systems can beneficially embed automated learning within virtually any type of business *process*, delivering the learning to users in the form of *adaptive recommendations* of many different varieties.
5. As people interact with the system, and additional knowledge and systems are integrated within this adaptive network, a fundamentally new system-based capability emerges: the *learning layer,* which evolves to become an integral part of the fabric of an organization.
6. The productivity and competitive advantages of the learning layer are such that wide-scale implementation of this technology is inevitable; it will drive the next major wave of enterprise IT, and it will be an imperative for *your* business.

It should be pretty apparent that this book describes an *emerging* leading practice (in more ways than one), not a currently established best practice. It is not just a basic idea or two inflated up to book size through the liberal use of anecdotes and concocted cases. Rather, it is a set of recently invented and integrated ideas—ideas woven together into an inevitable whole—that I think you will agree are likely to have some profound ramifications for your organization.

And to kick-start your thinking on how you can take advantage of the learning layer in your own organization, the third part of the book highlights specific application areas that are relevant to the issues and directions of your particular organization. These application opportunities are put into the context of a business *fabric* framework, the fabric comprising an integration of strategy, capabilities, and culture. The fabric of a business should be capable of adapting over time. When it doesn't, performance suffers, and in the worst case, the business ultimately ceases to exist.

I think you will find this strategic tapestry, along with some related novel and broad-based *business renewal* processes, quite useful for thinking about the state of your business and alternative directions you might take—it is really a next generation approach for business strategy development. But here we are going to focus on its use as a means to explore the applications and implications of the learning layer. We will see that the learning layer facilitates the business fabric adapting in a way not previously possible, and we will explore a variety of specific examples of exactly how it can do this.

While the implications of the learning layer can be quite concrete, some of the subject matter is necessarily of a more abstract nature than is typical for the average business book. I make no apologies for that because in today's world, inventions, and progress most generally, primarily come from applying the power of abstraction in novel ways. But the book is meant to be highly accessible to time-constrained business executives, so I've tried to present the details of the logic path leading to the learning layer and its applications in a summarized and common sense manner.

For those readers primarily just interested in the way the learning layer works, its broad implications, and how to get started implementing, you can just skip some or all of the application discussion in Part III of the book. And the highly technical reader may be eager for a few more technological details—that's the next book!

Acknowledgments

This book has been a long time in the making, much less so in the writing—it pretty much wrote itself. It wrote itself because it really just chronicles the evolution of its namesake, the *learning layer*. That evolution has been for the most part on public display over the years at www.manyworlds.com, which serves as a business thought leadership hub, as well as a demonstration facility for some of the technical capabilities described in the book.

I want to first thank the thousands of manyworlds.com members, whose use of the site and suggestions for improvements benefited greatly the development of technologies that make the learning layer a reality. This book also owes much to the manyworlds.com thought leader network, extraordinary individuals who contributed wisdom to the site that has benefited me and my ManyWorlds colleagues, as well as the public. Special appreciation goes to Michael Schrage, Bob Sutton, Mohan Sawhney, John Hagel III, Art Kleiner, Nick Carr, John Sifonis, Robert Tucker, Hank Chesbrough, Tom Davenport, Clay Christensen, Renee Mauborgne, W. Chan Kim, Jane Linder, Jim Ericson, Michael Tanner, Ray Kurzweil, Steve Jurvetson, and J. Scott Armstrong.

Some of the systems experts who have helped build the ship that gradually became a platform capable of enabling the learning layer include Ryan Harris, Emlyn O'Regan, Qing Huo, Fernando Gekdyszman, Emiliano Parizzi, and Brian Roisentul. A special thanks to Max More, who has long sailed the ship while it was still being built—the ship is much the stronger for his feedback and guidance, as is the book itself.

And most of all, my gratitude to my coinventor of the learning layer, Naomi Moneypenny, who designed the ship and has long managed its construction, and who made this book possible.

I'd also like to thank my literary agent, Giles Anderson, who reached out to me about writing a book long before I had conceived of it, and thanks to the team at Palgrave Macmillan who made the book a reality.

And although the book "wrote itself," I appreciate my family allowing me to skip out on a few softball and volleyball games to "get r'done."

The Learning Layer

PART I

IMPERATIVE AND OPPORTUNITY

I

Introduction

The business thinker and author Arie de Geus is famous for the insight that ultimately a business's only sustainable competitive advantage is to learn to learn faster than the competition. That insight helped spawn a significant movement toward more effective organizational learning over the past couple of decades. The emphasis of this movement has been primarily on increasing learning effectiveness through examining and improving personal learning approaches, as well as facilitating more productive interactions with others.

Both de Geus and I are alumni of Royal Dutch Shell, and Shell has been at the forefront of exploring new methods of enhancing organizational learning since the 1970s. I was fortunate enough to have positions at Shell that involved testing and putting many of those organizational learning techniques into practice, techniques ranging from scenario development, systems thinking applications, and even gestalt psychology! It was quite rewarding—we made some significant impacts on business performance, and I got to hobnob with some very bright and interesting people from top consulting organizations and universities who brought these ideas to Shell, and who left with ideas that were all the stronger for being tempered in the crucible of actual practice.

However, in addition to having those fun and stimulating assignments that included roles in promoting more effective organizational learning within a wide variety of Shell businesses, I also had the bit more prosaic, as well as quite often thankless, role as a Chief Information Officer at Shell (yes, I guess you could say I'm still a recovering CIO . . .). That job, among myriad other duties, included responsibilities for knowledge management (KM) and technologies to support organizational learning. So I was made keenly aware, being on the receiving end of periodic eruptions of frustration, that the supporting technical infrastructure for organizational learning was not nearly as sophisticated as the people-based learning methods we were pioneering. Although the technical state of the art could enhance collaboration and improve access to information, it certainly had little to no innate ability to learn, or even to directly facilitate learning. The venting of frustration was somewhat muted from what it would have otherwise been because, of course, no one seriously expected systems to have any innate learning ability. Expectations had been suitably dashed on that score long ago.

But through all of the expectation booms and busts, technical progress does inevitably march on. It is now time, tempered by hard-knocks realism, to ratchet up our expectations again—the next era of information technology (IT) has begun to creep up on us, and learning is at its core. It has generally gone unnoticed, or perhaps has just been drowned out in the daily noise of technology news streams, but we have entered the era of *adaptation*. On the Internet we have already begun to expect that the systems we interact with will to some degree adapt to our specific needs—that is, we have increasingly come to expect these Internet systems to learn about us and respond accordingly. That expectation, and its fulfillment, promises to become universal.

The Third Wave

In fact, to put this into a broader historical perspective, a case can be made that the era of adaptation, when viewed most fundamentally, represents only the *third* wave of IT since the inception of computing (figure 1.1). The first wave spanned the initial decades of the IT industry, in which the primary

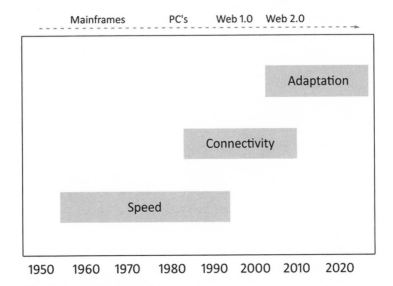

Figure 1.1 Waves of IT

bottleneck was processing *speed*. Bigger, faster mainframes were developed in this era, followed by personal computers and servers that allowed more distributed and responsive processing capabilities. That transition effectively ended the battle. Only in exceptional, highly specialized situations is processing speed a limiting factor for what we want to get done today.

In the subsequent couple of decades of computing, *connectivity* was more often the limiting factor. Of course, the big story of the Internet is that it has been the solution to most of the connectivity bottlenecks that once so bedeviled applications of IT. Anyone with any connection at all to the Internet can reach just about any other person or system that is connected to the Internet. The Internet has enabled e-commerce, vastly easier publishing, more extensive people-to-people connections, and all the creative destruction that has come with it. It has helped make the "network" the default structure for just about anything we think about, whether business or science. It's almost hard to remember what it was like before the Internet, even though it was not so many years ago.

The Internet not only solved the problem of connectivity, but also provided the foundation for the next mega wave of IT, *adaptation*. The Internet laid the groundwork for the era of adaptation in two very fundamental ways. First, by virtue of being able to connect together a wider range of users, the Internet enables systems to access a broader base of user experiences with which to work, from which to *learn*. Adaptive features were introduced in a few applications of the initial commercial phase of the Internet, and have become more prevalent in the more recent "Web 2.0" era. These features are typically still fairly limited in learning ability, however, and remain primarily the province of consumer product sites. To be sure, we are only at the very beginning of the adaptation wave.

The second fundamental way the Internet laid the groundwork for the era of adaptation is a bit more subtle, and will be addressed in much detail and from various angles throughout this book. It is the fact that the Internet shifted the default thinking on systems structures to the *network* rather than the hierarchy. In fact, this paradigm shift from hierarchies to networks of the past ten or so years has affected much more than just computing. The very lens through which wide swaths of science is viewed has suddenly become highly sensitive to the presence of networks.[1] Where we could see only hierarchies before, we now see rich sets of networks. And there is quite likely a reason that seemingly everywhere we look in nature, we now see networks—as we will see, network structures are a *necessity* for truly adaptive systems, and nature is surely that.

Is adaptation truly the next big thing? After all, a new next big thing seems to be trotted out by the IT community every few years. What about some other candidates for the next big wave of IT? Well, as one prominent example, *cloud computing* gets a good deal of press these days. It is basically the concept of hiding the physical details of computing from the user and making computing costs totally variable rather than fixed. It too is surely an inevitable trend, but it's not really going to be transformational for most businesses. It promises to reduce costs and increase flexibility. But by its very nature of being a commodity, it will not enable competitive advantages.

There is also certainly an increasing trend toward greater reliance on mobile devices, but the ubiquity of mobile computing, by itself, is not likely to be transformational for most businesses. But when coupled with capabilities for adaptation it may well be; the mind boggles at the possibilities for highly adaptive mobile devices. Adaptation appears to stand alone as the big, inevitable IT trend that also will really matter for most businesses.

By the way, why not call our third wave of IT "intelligent" technology rather than "adaptive" technology? Intelligent is surely the broader term, but its very broadness dilutes its usefulness. Adaptive, on the other hand, is specific enough to be usefully explanatory, and in fact, is likely to be the most important way enhanced intelligence will be built into systems for the foreseeable future. More specifically, what we mean by adaptive is the ability to *learn from experience*. And learning from experience in the context of adaptive systems primarily means learning from the system's experiences with *people* or their works.

The business implications of this "adaptive world" have only begun to be explored, however. It is not widely recognized, for example, but the common denominator of arguably the two most successful companies of the Internet era to date, Google and Amazon, is that each uniquely exploited adaptive technologies based on the *patterns of behaviors* of people, to accelerate past their competition in their respective spaces. Google's initial search engine superiority rested on its unique leverage of a form of social information, the patterns of purposively created hyperlinks that were embedded in sites all across the Web. Amazon was a highly successful pioneer in generating recommendations based on customer purchase patterns that serve to drive increased sales. So the early winners at applying the power of adaptation at large scales not coincidentally also won the war of shareholder value in round one of the Internet. But the future *is* unevenly distributed—for most businesses, the opportunities and threats lie ahead.

Why then has this emerging revolution in IT had such a relatively low profile with business in general? First, it is algorithm and data driven, so its operations are arcane and somewhat hidden. Second, it has been pioneered by e-commerce and advertising business models that have so far affected a fairly narrow business segment. And perhaps most importantly, after the go-go years of the 1990s, many businesses outside of the e-commerce area have basically gone to sleep with regard to potentially transformational IT. They have bought into the story that IT is primarily just a commodity now—that it no longer can serve to create competitive advantages. And, in fact, IT does go through periods of incremental advances with little in the way of strategic implications for most organizations. So yes, the IT slumber of the better part of the last decade may have been warranted—but it is now time to heed the alarm clock!

So How Is This Different Than . . . ?

There are a couple of framing questions that naturally arise with regard to this new IT era of adaptation, and the associated technologies and approaches discussed in this book. The first question is, "Isn't this just Web 2.0?" And the answer is that it *is* the logical and *integrated* extension of the philosophy of Web 2.0. "Web 2.0" is not a very crisply defined term, but certainly a core theme is the leveraging of collective intelligence, or as more colorfully and memorably put by James Surowiecki, leveraging "the wisdom of the crowd."[2] The era of adaptation will certainly fully embrace the leveraging of collective intelligence, but to better illustrate the ways it will extend what Web 2.0 has begun, let's do a quick overview of the major categories of Web 2.0 technologies.

The first set of technologies that would generally be attributed to Web 2.0 are blogs and wikis—fundamentally easier ways to *publish*, and thereby enabling many more people to get information and their opinions out to others. Blogs are typically a single author doing the publishing, whereas wikis are collective publishing and editing, but the common feature is ease of participation in the world of publishing. Twitter is the latest twist on this—a platform that enables *micro* blogging in real time.

Another set of technologies attributed to Web 2.0 are those that enable people to organize and reference information, or to provide their perspectives, for the benefit of others. The communal tagging of content with keywords is a good example of this. And other "wisdom-of-the-crowd" features commonly associated with Web 2.0 include community rating of content or people, providing communal answers to questions, and gaining collective views of the future through polling or information markets.

What all of these themes of Web 2.0 have in common is the more broad-based leverage of community knowledge than was prevalent in the systems that came before them. Often this wisdom of the crowd is *directly consumed* by a user, but it can also first be processed by the system and summarized for consumption, or in the most sophisticated applications, serve as the basis for intelligent search and recommendations.

The other broad thematic thread underpinning Web 2.0 is the rise of online social networking. The representation of people and their relationships within a system constitutes an entirely different computing perspective from that of previous eras. It's sort of the Copernican revolution in reverse—the center of the computing universe moves from "out there" to the individual. And while being more centered on the individual, the social networking paradigm at the same time tends to promote a new kind of individual identity—an individual becomes *defined* by her particular network of relationships as the relationships become increasingly transparent to her, as well as to others.

The overall approach and supporting technical capabilities described in this book extend beyond these classic Web 2.0 concepts in two important ways. First, there is an architectural preference and capability for *integrating* otherwise disparate Web 2.0-type functions, and also integration with existing business systems—meaning, for example, that content management, social networking, and "wisdom of the crowd" capabilities should not be consigned to artificially separated systems. Second, there is much more emphasis on the capacity for sophisticated and automated *learning* from the behavioral information accessible within this integrated environment. In fact, Web 2.0-type applications are sometimes categorized under the much more useful and descriptive term "social computing." The approach described in this book fully embraces the term "social computing," and by virtue of the automated learning capabilities it brings to bear, as opposed to classic Web 2.0 applications, it pays more than just lip service to the "computing" part of the term.

So this book describes what I believe is the inevitable conclusion of Web 2.0—call it Web X.0, in which "X" is whatever digit greater than two you would care to give it. It particularly addresses an issue McKinsey & Co. highlighted in a recent report on Web 2.0 implementations in enterprises: "Participatory technologies have the highest chance of success when incorporated into a user's daily workflow."[3] That is, if a business user needs to make an extra effort to put information into a stand-alone wiki or a blog, initial enthusiasm will inevitably peter out and long-term results will be disappointing. In contrast, the integrated and automated approach outlined in this book actually *does* embed the act of informing, as well as the act of learning, within the daily workflow.

The broader issue at play here is that what works well on the Web in general will *not* necessarily work as well *within* a company. One reason is because there is a different "cost of time" dynamic. Participation, and particularly meaningful contributions that are of an unpaid nature, is a manifestation of a user segment with relatively low cost of time. Such a segment is relatively rare in most business organizations, at least while on the job. Certainly, the romantic in us wistfully wants to believe that work is a labor of love for everyone in the organization all of the time, but I think we all know the reality is different. Some people will certainly, because of inclination or lower cost of time, do more of the heavy lifting of contributing than others within an organization—we just should not be Pollyanas about the level that will be sustained without integration within a workflow, and without clear incentives.

A second question that arises in putting the book's subject into context is, "How is all of this different than artificial intelligence (and I thought AI was dead)?" Well, to the extent that the systems that will be described include learning algorithms and thereby act intelligently, they can be considered a type of AI. But AI is such a broad concept as to be basically meaningless in the context of today's systems. If we are going to use the acronym AI in this context, better to have it stand for "adaptive intelligence." This is more precise because the system's intelligence is really just the ability to amplify the intelligence of people in ways that are personally useful. Plus, we are not talking about Arthur C. Clarke's HAL 9000-type artificial intelligence here—we need to avoid the unrestrained expectations that the term AI has been prone to in the past. We *are* talking about more intelligent and useful systems, but we also don't want to get too carried away.

But I want to reemphasize that it is the advent of the Internet that is the advance that makes the era of broad-based adaptation possible. Not necessarily a *direct* result of the Internet, but indirectly due to paradigm shifts in system structure and functions that the Internet represents, and that it enables. The first paradigm shift is that the network structure is king. All other structures play a subordinate role. This seems almost obvious now. But look around your business and see if most of your IT systems yet embrace this shift. There is a long way to go in harnessing the power of the network. And the second shift is the recognition that people's behaviors as they go about their daily work represent a vast, untapped resource. AI techniques have been around for quite a while, but when coupled with the power and flexibility of networks, and attention to collective behaviors, we get the necessary ingredients for the new IT era of adaptation.

So this book just describes an inevitable evolution. Evolution always works by building on what comes before it. We will see how embracing a wisdom-of-the-crowd approach quite naturally leads to *socially aware* systems. And these socially aware systems can be extended to learn from their awareness and deliver the learning back to people in the form of recommendations of many kinds. And taken to its ultimate conclusion, the socially aware system can also make recommendations to *itself*, applying its learning to quite literally reconfigure itself, and by extension our work processes, on an ongoing basis. And by integrating these new capabilities across, and within, a network of our existing systems and process infrastructure, something entirely new emerges: a layer of learning that enables us all to work much smarter.

These, then, are the series of steps that will lead us into the era of adaptation, and also to the inevitable outcome of building learning into the very fabric of your business in a way never before possible!

2

Intellectual Capital Acceleration: The Competitive Imperative

The company I founded and work for, ManyWorlds, is a bit of an odd beast—we're basically a design company, but somewhat unusually, our designs lie at the intersection of business and technology. We design (and build) systems, but we also help businesses design and implement strategies and processes.

So I've had the privilege of working with a good number of leading multinational corporations, and their very capable leaders, on their strategic directions. In the course of this kind of work, I routinely ask the executives of these companies what they think their advantages are versus their competitors who have not enjoyed quite as much success. Invariably the answers revolve in some way around the concept of intellectual capital. In many cases they will emphasize that their advantages derive from their people (the human capital part of intellectual capital). Sometimes I will get an answer that suggests the advantage is due to the company's superior processes. Sometimes it is their technology. But in nearly all cases it boils down to *know-how*, whether embodied in people or in knowledge that is in some sense institutionalized.

Even for companies I've worked with that are highly capital intensive, it is usually not the steel-on-the-ground that provides the ultimate advantage, but rather it is the know-how that was applied to put the right type of steel-on-the-ground at the right time and in the right place that led to the financial rewards. So although they may couch it in a variety of terms, it is pretty well accepted by most executives these days that building and managing their intellectual capital is at the heart of their long-term business performance.

The intuition of business executives is generally pretty good. And the intuitive recognition by executives that know-how, and the organizing and managing of know-how, is at the core of their competitiveness is well supported by detailed examination of the drivers of financial performance across companies and industries. For example, an analysis highlighted in the recent book *Mobilizing Minds* provides compelling evidence that a company's success versus peers can be directly attributed to the company's ability to generate excess returns from the "thinking-intensive" portions of their workforce.[1] In particular, the authors demonstrate that it is the ability to overcome the higher complexity levels of increased workforce size while still enjoying the rewards of greater scale that is a key factor in separating the most successful businesses from the others.

These conclusions are amplified by the even more recent research of John Hagel III, John Seely Brown, and Lang Davison, which is summarized in their article, "The Big Shift: Measuring the Forces of Change"[2]—the title referring to a fundamental shifting in the way business value is created in today's economy. They point out that "[a]s stability gives way to change and uncertainty, institutions must increase not just efficiency but also the rate at which they learn and innovate, which in turn will boost their rate of performance improvement." And they reach a key conclusion about a business's path to successful value creation that echoes the findings of *Mobilizing Minds*: that increasingly " 'scalable efficiency' . . . must be replaced by 'scalable learning.' "

Of course, the ability to learn effectively was always the paramount concern of perhaps the most effective CEO of the past generation, Jack Welch, as he worked to turbocharge the performance of GE, the very archetype of the large and complex company that presents the greatest scalable learning challenge. Welch, coming to essentially the same conclusion as Arie de Geus, famously stated that "... an organization's ability to learn, and translate that learning into action rapidly, is the ultimate competitive advantage."[3]

The Reality Gap

So perhaps highlighting the importance of intellectual capital and organizational learning amounts to belaboring the obvious—intellectually business leaders clearly get it, and any number of economic and financial analyses confirm it. But there is a reality gap because leaders haven't had a meaningful way to link learning to hard business performance metrics. And frankly, having been there, like it or not, the reality is that if something isn't measurable in terms that ultimately translate into a credible, financially based indicator, it is not going to get serious senior executive attention. In today's business environment, this measurement gap simply can no longer be tolerated. As Hagel, Brown and Davison stress in "The Big Shift": "Companies must therefore design and track operational metrics showing how well they participate in knowledge flows."

The good news is that as we journey to the learning layer and its applications, we will find that new, powerful, and credible metrics associated with intellectual capital and learning will be automatic by-products. These are metrics that put the value of learning and knowledge on as firm a ground as that of any hard asset—*hard data* not being solely reserved for *hard assets* any longer. This will serve to better balance your business's investments by enabling you to develop a truly comprehensive value "dashboard" that supports the investment agenda you know to be intuitively right, but for which you have not had the hard, credible data required that would facilitate others in drawing the same conclusions.

Another manifestation of the intellectual capital and learning reality gap is that when you ask executives, who, or at least what organization, in their company has the overall responsibility for the management of intellectual capital in their businesses, you tend to get a blank stare. After a long pause, they are likely to say something like, "Well, if you mean how we provide onboarding and ongoing training and education programs for our people, that's Human Resources." Another typical answer you will hear is, "Information about our customers is absolutely critical for our business, and our IT organization manages our customer databases and data mining systems." Or occasionally you'll get something along the lines of, "Legal manages our intellectual property." So is it HR, IT, Legal, or somewhere else?

The confusion about responsibility for companies' knowhow and the lack of a holistic approach can lead to an insidious erosion of the capacity for intellectual capital growth. And at times it is worse than that—it spells the actual *loss* of critical know-how. The recent period of economic turmoil is a good case in point. I have personally witnessed businesses rapidly, typically in panic mode, mothballing significant projects and initiatives. Yes, they have attempted to archive their content and models as they slash their workforce. But they have lost so much of the context and other information locked up in the minds of the departed that a graceful restart will be impossible. And in some businesses there are other time bombs working against them. Workforces with much of their expertise residing in staff who are within a few years of retirement or staff who are ready to jump to happier hunting grounds elsewhere if the stock price dips face a know-how drain that is analogous in effect to facing an unrelenting series of widespread layoffs.

A good deal of the difficulty in getting a handle on effectively managing intellectual capital is to a large degree a symptom of it being simultaneously a big and a very slippery concept. What is *it* exactly? And how does it relate to knowledge and to learning? And what is organizational learning all about, as opposed to just individual learning? It looks like we'll need to briefly sort through some abstractions that are piled on top of yet more abstractions to make some sense of it.

Maybe we should take a look at a workable definition of a learning organization. The best definition I've seen is one that David Garvin develops in his book *Learning in Action* on the basis of his survey and consideration of a number of earlier definitional candidates:[4]

> A learning organization is an organization skilled at creating, acquiring, interpreting, transferring, and retaining knowledge, and at purposefully modifying its behavior to reflect new knowledge and insights.

Several key points stand out from Garvin's definition of a learning organization. First, the *generation* of new knowledge or insights is considered an essential feature. Second, this knowledge must be *transferred* and *retained*. And third, the knowledge needs to be put into *practice*. So learning is a function of *actions* with regard to *knowledge*.

The Math of Learning

But what exactly are the relationships of these concepts at their most fundamental level? Let's boil it down even more, by bringing some math to bear on the topic, of all things! Specifically, let's see if we can take these concepts and connect the dots with business performance by dusting off our calculus.[5] Here goes: we can start with the fact that learning clearly implies an increase in knowledge, or most broadly speaking, intellectual capital. So more formally, knowledge is a *stock*—in theory you can measure it in *absolute* terms at any point in time. Learning, on the other hand, is a *flow*. As a flow, learning is the measure of the *difference* between stocks of knowledge at two different points in time.

In other words, in the terms of calculus, learning is the *derivative* with respect to time of the knowledge "function."

Inversely, cumulating (or in calculus terms, *integrating*) learning over a period of time yields a stock of knowledge. So in Newtonian terms, knowledge is analogous to distance, and learning is analogous to velocity.

If you prefer accounting to calculus, you can think of knowledge as the balance sheet and learning as the income statement. And yes, if you are wondering, unfortunately you can have negative net learning, just like you can have negative net income!

Ok, simple enough. But even this little excursion into calculus delivers some insights. For example, it makes really clear just how *inseparable* the management of a business's knowledge is from learning processes, even though many organizations seem to try their hardest to keep them separate.

Let's go one step further and close the loop with the some of the key points in the Introduction. Recall Arie de Geus's insight that the only sustainable competitive advantage is to learn to learn faster than the competition. Learning to learn faster? Let's see, that is the change in the *rate* of learning, meaning the derivative of learning, or the second derivative of knowledge. In Newtonian terms that's analogous to a change in velocity, which equals acceleration! So sustainable competitive advantage equals the first derivative of learning, which equals the second derivative of intellectual capital—or in other words, and loosely speaking, the *acceleration of intellectual capital.*

It makes sense when you think about it—the great human advances have all revolved around infrastructure that has enabled learning to learn better. Language, writing, the Internet, all fit in that category of breakthrough infrastructure. These are the kinds of infrastructure that serve to not just increase but to *increase the rate of increase* in the stock of knowledge and understanding.

The imperative, then, is to turn the equation of sustainable competitive advantage into reality, not just a quaint slogan. We need to find the levers that really do accelerate intellectual capital development. And clearly our math suggests the levers must lie at the intersection of the fields of organizational learning, cognitive science, information and knowledge management, and IT. And those are indeed the fields through which our journey here shall take us.

Hidden in Plain Sight

Let's return to the organizational issues of intellectual capital management now that we have a basic sense of the relationship between learning and knowledge (or intellectual capital). HR organizations, and specifically organizational effectiveness (OE) groups, have a strong orientation toward learning, which is, as we saw, all about the generation of positive change in intellectual capital. In particular, the emphasis of HR is on increasing the *human capital* portion of intellectual capital. Makes sense—HR people are, after all, *people* people; they tend to be personally oriented toward learning and development. IT, on the other hand, is all about managing intellectual capital that is embodied in systems. So IT is about the stock of knowledge, and HR is about the flow of learning.

And, of course, as all of us who have worked in a company of any size know, the twain rarely meets among these leaders of the management of the firm's intellectual capital. Because—let's face it—sometimes there is a grain of truth in stereotypes. It is not much of an exaggeration to say that the organizational effectiveness part of HR often only grudgingly deals with IT systems—typically limited to, for example, applications that manage training programs. And IT often doesn't understand the whole people thing at all—but they sure know about things such as databases, data mining, remote access, and content management systems.

So is the barrier to get to the next level of organizational learning performance a cultural divide—*people* people versus bit fiddlers? No, the problem is that there are some blind spots in our frame of reference. And at the risk of being painted as a management consultant type, let me introduce

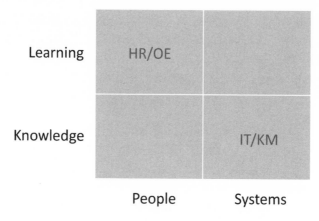

Figure 2.1 The Intellectual Capital Acceleration Opportunity Matrix

a simple little two-by-two intellectual capital acceleration opportunity matrix (figure 2.1) to illustrate the point.

Aligned with my admittedly rather sweeping categorizations, on the opportunity matrix HR/OE is aligned with people learning more effectively, and IT and KM are all about knowledge embodied in systems. Ok, so there is nothing terribly insightful about that. But wait—that's only *half* of the matrix! What about the other two glaringly blank quadrants? They don't get nearly as much attention—perhaps none at all.

Well, in the lower left quadrant we have the *tacit* knowledge or intellectual capital residing solely within people's heads. Businesses for the most part assume that just *is*. Other than maybe recruiting, there aren't specific processes and organizations for addressing this pool of tacit know-how. If people bother to *overtly* communicate their knowledge within the realm of computer systems, then IT can manage that, and it ends up in the lower right quadrant of our two-by-two matrix. Or if people overtly teach others, they can directly contribute to the learning of other people, which is the upper left quadrant. Otherwise, without overt actions, knowledge in people's heads just *is*—a blank quadrant that is hidden in plain sight.

Then there is the blank upper right quadrant. And to clarify, that quadrant is not about systems that *support* people's learning—any system that embodies or helps to transmit knowledge in the lower right quadrant can do that. I'm talking about systems that actually learn. This quadrant is blank because, as I mentioned in the Introduction, nobody really expects *that* to be possible to any significant extent.

But what this book is all about is demonstrating that there are, in fact, some new answers for both of these blank quadrants. That knowledge and insights within the heads of people can be leveraged without them overtly taking actions to make it so. And that systems can actually learn, and more specifically, learn from *latent* intellectual capital. Clay Shirky has popularized the term "cognitive surplus" with regard to the societal dividend associated with the mass migration from time spent passively watching TV to time spent actively participating in the Internet.[6] In businesses, there has presumably not been the time-wasting equivalent of TV watching going on, but what has been occurring is a cognitive surplus that has gone untapped because there was not the means or the time available to tap into it.

But now we *have* the means to fully address the other half of the matrix, and by filling in those blank quadrants, we gain an entirely new lever for enabling an organization to learn to learn better—that is, to accelerate intellectual capital (figure 2.2).

So that's our challenge in chart form—and it shockingly implies that our goal will be to unleash the entire other half of the value of intellectual capital in your organization that has been hidden in plain sight for so long. But how are we going to actually make it happen? Well, we're going to take it one step at a time. And those steps are going to culminate in the phenomenon that we will come to call the *learning layer*. This learning layer will be revealed to be an ethereal web of learning residing above standard systems infrastructure that will tap the cognitive surplus, and amplify its effects across your organization. And that will lead to possibilities

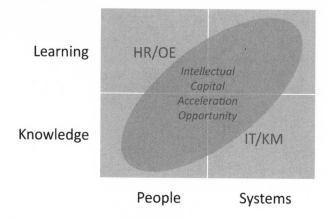

Figure 2.2   The Opportunity Target

for attaining a whole new level of business productivity and sustainable advantage.

There really is no other way to get to those higher level of productivities to which we all aspire. A perspective attributed to Jack Welch on what it takes to win the race for performance improvement, couched in the context of comparing the 1990s with the 1980s, readily applies, perhaps even more so, to our own times: "The 1980s will seem like a walk in the park when compared to new global challenges, where annual productivity increases of 6% may not be enough. A combination of software, brains, and running harder will be needed to bring that percentage up to 8% or 9%." The running harder part you will have to take care of. The combination of software and brains is where the learning layer quite literally comes in.

PART II

THE LEARNING LAYER

3

Lessons from the Brain

As the father of a teenager I have had the wonderful opportunity to be reminded on a daily basis for a good many years the remarkable way the human brain develops and adapts. Yes, there is learning, but there is more—there is an inherent plasticity that allows the brain to do much more than just learn by rote. An interwoven base of learning and an overall personality evolves, and it all evolves in some ways that are fairly predictable, but in other ways that are completely unpredictable.

And then there are our computer systems. As I type this, my word processing system is not learning much of anything as far as I can tell. There is no development of a personality over time. It does not suddenly surprise me with a nugget of insight every now and then.

For many years, of course, we've tried to build computer systems that are more than just obedient idiots. It has turned out to be a very hard problem—much harder than early computer scientists had imagined, and certainly much harder than science fiction writers had conceived. For one thing, people were initially fooled because they underestimated just how much we humans really do *know*—they thought that human-type knowledge could be encoded in an admittedly large, but still manageable, body of programmed rules. It turns out that you needed a vastly larger tangle of rules than was ever imagined to create what would be viewed as an intelligent system in anything other than a very niche application area. The bigger stumbling block, however, was the issue of how additional rules would be added over time without people going to the trouble of doing the adding. This is where the rule-based approach broke down. And without this ability, there could be no automatic learning.

So how do we build a system that actually learns? We could do worse than take a lesson from the one "machine" that we definitely know has the capability of learning: the brain. We're not going to rival the learning power of the human brain any time soon, but maybe we can learn something important from how the brain does it. And just how *does* the brain do it? Well, we don't know *exactly*—the details remain a subject of very active research and will for a very long time to come. But here is something very fundamental that we do know: the most basic architectural feature of the brain is that it is essentially a giant network, where the nodes of the brain network are neurons. And it is a very large network indeed— the human brain contains on the order of about one hundred billion (10^{11}) neurons with about one hundred trillion (10^{14}) connections.

The connections among neurons are made at junctions called synapses, and each neuron is typically connected to thousands of other neurons. Neurons communicate with other neurons at these synaptic junctions by releasing neuro-transmitters that travel across the junctions. The cumulative effect on a receiving neuron of these chemical communi-cations is a change in its electrical potential. When this potential reaches a certain threshold, it causes the neuron to "fire," setting off pulses of communications to other neurons, which in turn may be caused to fire, and so on. Neuronal communications are thereby cascaded throughout the neural network, resulting in highly complex patterns of collective interactions.

Another thing we know about the brain is that the *strength* of the communications among networks of neurons is better modeled as an *analog* rather than *digital* process. In other words, the connections of the brain network are weighted across a potential continuum of values rather than just being binary, "1 or 0" or "yes or no," in nature. This implies that all representations in the brain are, at the most basic level, composed of weighted networks. This makes intuitive sense given that the brain has to continuously and effectively deal with all of the ambiguities and inherent fuzziness of the world around us.

We don't find obvious hierarchical structures, for example, in these most basic structural elements of the brain.[1] Rather, the brain uses the versatility of the weighted network structures upon which it is built to represent hierarchies, logic, and all the other synthetic, non-fuzzy constructs that populate our intellectual lives. The brain also relies on this architecture to do more than just *represent* aspects of the world around us; it also uses this structure to make the difficult daily stream of *choices* required in the face of the noisiness, the uncertainties, and the fuzziness of our world. Recent research in the field of cognitive science has concluded that our choices are never completely black and white, and made with complete confidence.[2] The research concludes that "even a binary choice leaves in its wake a quantity that represents degree of belief." So we have a "machine" with degrees of belief and weightings layered one on top of another, all made possible by the versatility of its underlying weighted network structure.

A Network Evolving

That's the architectural basics of the brain, but how does the brain actually learn? Although many of the details remain to be understood, we know that, fundamentally, learning in the brain is a function of adding, deleting, strengthening, and weakening the connections among neurons. This modification of the weighted network that is our brain occurs continuously throughout our lives on the basis of experiences. Some events serve to reinforce historical experiences, and the brain network modifies itself by increasing the strength of network connections that in some way correspond to these experiences. On the other hand, when there is little experiential reinforcement over a long period of time, corresponding connections may weaken.

Some other new discoveries from the field of cognitive science suggest that there are certain times in which the modification of the vast network that is our brain is particularly intense. For example, during the downtime of particular stages of sleep, the brain seems to most intensely reshape itself. This may be why sleep deprivation has been shown to be anathema to learning. And this may also be why a requirement for sleep is universal among animals with brains. Even insects are known to require sleep, for example. Sleep may well be a necessity for effective learning—resulting from the reshaping network connections—to occur.[3]

That's the daily learning cycle. An analogous, but more comprehensive, phenomenon also occurs over a much longer time scale. During the first years of life, the human brain grows rapidly and trillions of new connections are formed among neurons. It takes fully 60 percent of a newborn's total energy requirements to accomplish this dramatic development.[4] It is a period of intense learning, and within a few years all of the basic faculties and skills that make us human are well in place. By puberty, the brain has reached about an adult level in size. Then, during the adolescent portion of our life the brain actively and judiciously trims many of the connections that were prevalent from our very early childhood (scientists call this "synaptic pruning"). But something more subtle also occurs. New connections are generated during the teenage years between the more widely separated parts of the brain.[5] So the net effect of this period of transition from the mind of the child to the mind of the adult is a brain with fewer connections, but with additional nonlocal connections.[6] And that is likely the reason why researchers are increasingly confirming what we parents already know—that a teenager's mind in many ways really *does* work fundamentally differently from an adult's!

We can speculate that perhaps the innate curiosity and creativity that we associate with childhood is due to this richer set of connections that we are all endowed with in our early years, but by trimming many of these connections and then adding some connections to more disparate brain functions, nature delivers an adult mind that has a stronger ability to focus on things that are (or at least were to our ancestors) most important for survival. In any event, the brain network is clearly shaped on both a near-term, daily basis and over much longer periods of one's life.

Nature does not do complex, very energy costly, and risky things unless there is a good reason to do so. And its reshaping of the brain is all of those things. As an example of the risks of reshaping, there is evidence that schizophrenia, a condition that typically manifests itself in the teenage years, occurs when the process of the pruning of network connections in the brain goes awry.[7] But nature does all of its complex brain shaping for one very good reason that trumps all the downsides—to enable the most effective learning possible.

Something else we know about the brain is that the modifications to the brain network cannot just be very simple correspondences to experiences. There is undoubtedly some of that type of simple learning for very constrained stimulus and response situations (e.g., Pavlovian responses), but more generally the brain seems to apply certain parts of the brain network to determine how and to what extent to modify other parts of the brain structure. In other words, there is an internal feedback loop at work, in addition to just very simple, direct responses to external experiences. This dynamic, working in conjunction with the vastness of the brain network, imparts to the learning process of the brain its high degree of complexity and consequent unpredictability. And from this dynamical interplay and consequent *evolving* of the brain network comes the brain's wonderful capacity for creativity—the ability to generate a continuing stream of novel perspectives, insights, and constructs.

You can easily see that feedback dynamic at work whenever you awaken from a dream. If you don't try to remember the dream, you will almost always forget it. But if you *will* yourself to recall more details of it, and then remember it, you can make the memory of the dream consolidate, potentially forever. When you do so, one part of your brain literally physically affects another part of your brain, which in turn may later influence other parts of your brain, and so on, for the rest of your life. Your mind will never be quite the same because of that little whim to remember that particular dream!

So the brain reshapes itself on a daily basis, as well as over our lifetimes, all for the sake of better learning. But we can pursue this temporal dimension of the reshaping of the brain *much* further by considering the way the human brain has *evolved* over the past few millions of years. Evolution always works by building on what comes before it, and the rapid expansion in hominid brain size was no different. This process has culminated in an additional layer of densely networked neurons called the neocortex, which lies over the top of the more ancient portions of our brains. This relatively thin sheet of extra learning power has such a large surface area in humans that it has to be severely folded so that it can fit in our skull and so that the connections among its neurons and those of the "ancient brain" below it are sufficiently close. This folded, extra layer of richly connected neurons is what gives the human brain its peculiarly convoluted look, and provides us humans with our uniquely powerful learning capabilities: all of the language abilities, social skills, logical reasoning, creativity, and powers of abstraction that are not found elsewhere in nature. The neocortex is nature's solution to the imperative of learning to learn better.

Ok, but what does all of this have to do with building learning into the fabric of your business? Well, our brief examination of the workings of the brain suggests that if we want an integrated organization of people and systems that effectively learns, we should start with a focus on a *network-based architecture* that has the capacity to *reshape itself* over time and that is *layered* over what came before it, because that's how the brain does it.

4

The Architecture of Learning

Here's a rhetorical question if there ever was one: have you ever had difficulty unraveling the mystery of where to find a needed item of information that you are pretty sure you saved electronically somewhere? Perhaps it's hard to even remember what form it was in—a presentation? Or was it in an article? Or did a colleague just casually mention it to you? Did you store it on your computer, and if so, which of the myriad folders could it be in? The search function may (or may not) help you. Often you have to try your best to retrace your steps chronologically or associatively, and that's hit or miss at best. Of course, the problem is that even though *you* are capable of learning and adapting (to the computer's way of doing things), your computer systems are not. When you consider all the time you and your colleagues waste looking for, or not even being aware of, items of relevance, the magnitude of the problem is clear.

A root cause of your difficulties is that the information you may be interested in often resides within *structures* that do not align with your particular context. So why can't the structures actually *adapt* so that they more often fit with your specific needs? The problem is that the most common structures used in IT are not sufficiently robust to support anything more than a very trivial level of adaptation. For example, the familiar hierarchical structures that store information in discrete folders or repositories do not have sufficient flexibility and inherent information storage capabilities to enable effective learning. For that, we need to take our lesson from the brain and apply a different architecture: the *fuzzy network.*

You probably remember the basics of standard set theory, which can be well represented by the familiar Venn diagrams (I use a few of those in this book). In this standard set theory, for which we ultimately have Aristotle to thank (or blame), an item either belongs to a set or it does not.[1] It is black and white; there are no shades of gray, no maybes. This application of our intellectual scalpel to the world allows us to build up logic structures and hierarchies that can be quite useful. The only problem is, sometimes, and perhaps *most* of the time, we need to deal with shades of gray. Items may mostly fit in one category, kind of fit in another category, tenuously fit in another, and so on.

We ran headlong into the tyranny of Aristotelian logic during the very early days of ManyWorlds. It was the dot com era; everything was possible, and we wanted to quickly create a state-of-the-art Internet portal for business thought leadership. It would include a number of topics that focused on aspects of strategy, business models, knowledge and learning, innovation, et cetera. To get started, we had a bunch of books that we had reviewed, and I had organized the books into a couple dozen separate stacks on a table in our little office. We had also come up with a starter set of 30 or so topical areas, and we wanted the books and some other content we had assembled to be mapped appropriately to the topics on the site. So I stuck a piece of paper on each stack of books that listed the set of topics to which the stacks should relate. In some cases it was a tough call, and I indicated the stacks only sort of fit with some of the listed topics. It all just seemed pretty natural and simple—what could be more straightforward to implement on a website, right?

It was clear from our simple mapping that the topics and books did not constitute any kind of strict hierarchy; so we were going to need a more flexible organizing structure. I asked my cofounder and chief technology officer (and the only person I had to delegate to at the time!) to find a web portal-generating system that could handle such a structure. We assumed that would be a pretty simple task—after all, it seemed to us that what we wanted to do must be a pretty commonplace requirement. She surveyed every possible commercial system available, but couldn't find a single one that could handle the job. After about the third time I asked her to look harder, somewhat reluctantly, we ended up building a system ourselves that could handle the job! That led us down a path of years of R&D, a bunch of patents, and ultimately this book—all born of a seemingly humdrum requirement and our naiveté of how simple it must be to address.

The good news for us was that we were able to successfully handle that initial little requirement and many larger versions of it because there is a more generalized set theory, called *fuzzy* set theory, that can explicitly handle the shades of gray. Fuzzy sets allow for full membership within a set just as in the case of standard sets, but they also allow for *partial* membership. Fuzzy sets are therefore the more general approach to categorization. They also tend to be more representative of the way the brain categorizes information. For every crisp hierarchy, there are hundreds of messy, fuzzy categorization problems of our everyday life that the brain seems to deal with just as effortlessly. So roll over Aristotle!

Fuzzy Networks

We can translate this fuzzy set paradigm to network structures in which the connections or relationships between nodes are *weighted* on a continuum rather than being digital, which is, as we saw, the same basic structure as that employed by the vast network that makes up the brain. We will call such a network a *fuzzy network*. That is, a fuzzy network is composed of nodes and weighted connections. And the connections may have specific *directions* and there may be more than one *type* of weighted connection between any given pair of nodes. This seems like a pretty simple concept, but most of the computer-based information structures that we are all familiar with are not fuzzy networks. Many are strict hierarchies. Or, as in the case of the relational databases that underpin the majority of modern business systems, they are not necessarily hierarchies but are still based firmly on standard, non-fuzzy set theory. The Internet itself is not a fuzzy network—it is a network, to be sure, but it is not *fuzzy* because the links between web pages are not weighted—rather, the links of the Web either exist or do not. There is no "sort of" with regard to hyperlinks among web pages.

Now, here is the important point: non-fuzzy networks as a practical matter can't really learn to any appreciable degree because there is insufficient flexibility and information storage within their structure to do so. Fuzzy networks, on the other hand, have the capability to learn by varying the weights of the links between nodes as required. A non-fuzzy network is really just a very constrained, and therefore limited, type of fuzzy network. If we normalize fuzzy network weightings on the 0-1 continuum, a non-fuzzy network (such as the Web) can be seen as just a fuzzy network constrained to "0" (no link) and "1" (a link exists) values. Because a fuzzy network relationship can take on potentially an infinite number of values versus only two values for the non-fuzzy network, the additional information storage, and hence learning, potential of the fuzzy network structure is clear (figure 4.1).

So it stands to reason if we want computer systems that can automatically learn we had better base them on fuzzy network structures. That's certainly not sufficient—we will also need some sophisticated auxiliary processing capabilities, but the fuzzy network structure is table stakes for building systems that can learn.

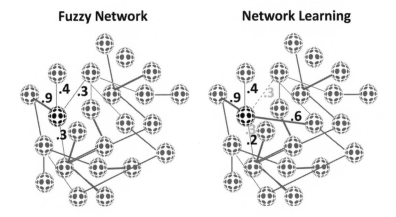

Figure 4.1   The Architecture of Learning

In the fuzzy network of the brain the nodes are neurons. In our computer-based fuzzy network structure they can be any type of system construct. For example, they can be web pages, blogs, documents, multimedia, or interactive applications. Although not a requirement, we may convert these chunks of raw information into what is often called in computing an "object" by putting a "wrapper" of descriptive information (sometimes called "meta-data") around the raw file or application. And these object-based nodes can consist of nothing more than some descriptive information and *pointers* to the actual files or applications referenced—the referenced information does not need to be embodied within the object itself. The fuzzy network can therefore take on a rather ethereal quality—consisting of just a dense web of fuzzy relationships and descriptive information.

Most generally, when implementing a fuzzy network to help manage the systems and work products of people in a business we can drop the computer jargon and just call these nodes something that sounds a little more directly relevant to business: "knowledge assets." This reinforces both the notion of their generality and that they have value, or at least potential value, to the organization—value that should be taken every bit as seriously as that of physical assets such as equipment in a plant.

In addition to these knowledge assets, some nodes may be special in that they represent *topical areas*. These are nodes that do not constitute a knowledge asset itself, but rather serve to provide descriptive information about a *collection* of knowledge assets that are *related* to it. In other words, these *topic* nodes derive their *meaning* by virtue of their relationships to knowledge assets, and through their relationships with other topics.

Certainly, there are many non-fuzzy quantities and relationships in the world of business information. For example, financial results are precise quantities, as are inventory levels. Products have specific parts lists. To help manage this non-fuzzy business world, business organizations have built up a non-fuzzy systems infrastructure that includes electronic spreadsheets, business intelligence systems, enterprise resource planning (ERP) systems, and customer relationship management (CRM) systems, to name just a few types of such systems. This non-fuzzy systems infrastructure will always be needed and will always be with us. But these systems don't learn to any appreciable degree, and the *processes* encompassing the systems certainly don't learn. The fuzzy network, our architecture of learning, can pick up where traditional systems leave off, surrounding these non-fuzzy legacy systems with a web of learning, thereby amplifying their value. A single neuron by itself can't do much. A fuzzy network of neurons can learn.

One of the advances in our understanding over the past 20 years or so is that we have learned the counterintuitive fact that highly complex phenomena can arise from fairly simple rules and constructs. Stephen Wolfram's work, highlighted in his book *A New Kind of Science*, for example, persuasively emphasizes and summarizes this point. And this perspective of "emergent" system properties resonates with what has long been known in the computer science community—that taking as a design starting point only minimal, essential foundations rather than introducing an array of ad hoc features yields the most elegant, extensible, and surprisingly powerful of systems.

So it is here. Seemingly almost by magic, just our two types of nodes, knowledge assets and topics, connected by fuzzy relationships, constitute a fuzzy network architecture that amazingly delivers all the power needed to serve as the foundation for automated organizational learning, applicable in a dizzying array of ways.

5

The End of Zombie Systems!

Here is a simple experiment you can perform with any young child.[1] Take a package of gum, secretly remove the gum, and replace it with something else, say, a small pencil. Then show the package of gum to the child and ask her what is in the package. After she gives the expected answer "gum," show her that there is actually a pencil inside. Now reclose the package with the pencil inside. After her mother, who has not seen any of this, comes into the room ask the child what her *mother* will say is in the package. Children around age four and older will typically think that their mother will say that there is gum in the package, because they will understand that their mother would have no basis for *not* thinking that. But children under the age of four will more typically think that their mother will say there is a pencil in the package. For these very young children, there is no "model" yet developed in their brain of a perspective other than their own.

Cognitive scientists refer to the ability to identify with the mental states of others as having a "theory of mind." It appears from testing other species that even the most basic elements of this capability are very rare in animals other than humans. It is also clear from our little experiment, and others like it, that humans are not born with this capability. Once again we find that the human brain *reshapes* itself—in this case in early childhood—to provide us with this remarkable facility, endowing each of us with a *social awareness* that effectively prepares us for the complexity of our social lives.

Recent research suggests that a necessary condition for developing a finely attuned social awareness is for the brain to have a wide-ranging and fully functional system of *mirror neurons*. Mirror neurons are special neurons that map the behaviors of others to brain subsystems that ordinarily apply to just the self. In other words, they provide the foundation for us to empathize, or more generally and informally, to put ourselves in the shoes of another. So they appear crucial for fully developing a theory of mind.[2]

If you think about it, historically computer systems have been totally devoid of anything like the mirror neurons that we have in our brains. Other than responding to deliberate interactions, there is no response to, much less learning from, the general, everyday behaviors of people interacting with the system. In fact, such behavioral information is not even *recognized*—systems have been completely oblivious to it. In this historic system paradigm, the user and the system are in a representational sense completely separate—there is not so much as a flicker of a theory of mind in the system that infers the interests and intentions of the user.

That is all about to change—the better than half-a-century era of socially *un*aware systems is coming to a close. The emerging standard paradigm for the new generation of systems is that usage behaviors, whether explicit or implicit, are captured and inferences on the mental states of the user are made from the collection of behaviors. These representations and inferences are continuously updated by the system as new behavioral information is received. In a representational sense, the people and the system "merge" in this new, adaptive paradigm (figure 5.1).

A system that is socially aware can do many new and truly wonderful things, not the least of which is to effortlessly learn to be increasingly useful to its users. We have been

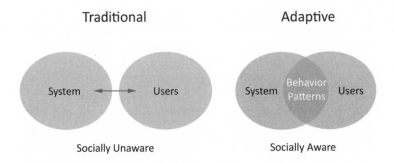

Figure 5.1 The Systems Paradigm Shift

so accustomed to socially unaware systems that it is almost hard to imagine how very unacceptable they will seem when viewed in the rear view mirror of the socially aware systems era. But imagine for a moment that you existed in a society in which absolutely no one responded to you unless you directly commanded someone to do something or asked someone a very specific question. And their responses to you are invariably direct—doing or saying nothing more or nothing less than required, not being able to infer or identify with any of your intentions, desires, preferences, or feelings. You would feel like you are in a bad zombie movie! But this "Night of the Living Dead" is exactly what we have come to accept with regard to our systems.

By the way, it is fascinating how very often new and useful concepts in one field have concurrent parallels in other fields. Just as the paradigm shift from hierarchy to network of the past decade has not been limited to applications in computing, but also has had a profound influence on other fields of science, so it is with behavioral awareness. Economists are as maligned as CIOs, and I should know as I am still in recovery from both professions, but believe it or not, economic models *are* getting better. And perhaps the key advance in economic theory of the last generation is the tossing out of the eminently rational "economic man" and replacing him in the models with an agent that exhibits the reality of human behaviors. The curtain has come down on the era of zombie economics as well as that of zombie systems!

Behaviors, Patterns, and Inferences

As mentioned in the Introduction, Web 2.0 has laid the groundwork for the socially aware systems paradigm. These Web 2.0 applications, each in their own unique way, have emphasized the leveraging of user behaviors reflecting collective wisdom to a much greater degree than the systems that came before them. In some of the applications, user ratings and feedback have been emphasized. Others have been focused on the collective tagging of information. Our socially aware system paradigm takes over where these Web 2.0 applications have left off by broadening the set of behaviors leveraged, beneficially categorizing and integrating the behaviors, and then applying more extensive and powerful analytical and inferencing capabilities to the collection of behaviors.

So what are the types of user behaviors that a socially aware system can recognize and apply? There can be a great many—some immediately applicable to just about any business environment, and others that will be more prevalent in future applications. Although numerous, the types of behaviors naturally fall into a manageable number of categories, and we will take a very brief look at each of these categories of behaviors.

We will start with the five categories comprising behaviors that can be attained with standard computers that are currently used in just about any business environment.

1. Navigation and Access Behaviors

The behaviors in this category relate to *navigating* through a system or trying to find information. For example, this category includes user access paths as determined by click streams, and can include transactional information, such as making a purchase. Also included in this category is performing search requests, as well as user responses to the results of a search request.

2. Collaborative Behaviors

This category encompasses behaviors with regard to *interactions* among people. It includes direct person-to-person communications (e.g., voice calls, e-mail, instant messages) or broadcasting behaviors, such as sending micro-blogs to a group of followers. This category also includes more indirect forms of communications (e.g., feedback on discussion forums). It includes the referral of content or people to other people. This category also includes the contributing, reviewing, and/or editing of information that others can access.

3. Reference Behaviors

Behaviors related to the *storing* or *organizing* of information for future reference personally or for the benefit of others are included in this category. So, for example, saving an item of content is a behavior in this category. Another example is tagging content so that it can be more easily found later. And the organizing *structure* a person uses to manage information that she intends to access later is a behavioral aspect included in this category.

4. Direct Feedback Behaviors

These are behaviors in which the user *directly* reveals preferences about *items* that are represented in the system. Examples of behaviors in this category include user ratings or comments associated with specific content or people. This includes, of course, direct feedback on recommendations that are generated by the system.

5. Self-Profiling and Subscription Behaviors

This category includes behaviors in which the user *directly* reveals information about *herself*. For example, indicating subscription preferences for specific areas of interest are included in this category. Information about oneself that is included in a user profile fits in this category. Examples of this type of self-profiling information are attributes such as age, gender, interests, affiliations.

These five categories of behaviors can be leveraged to create socially aware systems that can effectively learn in just about any current business environment.

There are at least two other categories of "behaviors" that require increasingly more sophisticated sensing capabilities, and that will therefore require enhanced interfaces beyond those that are typical in today's business computing environments. They are mentioned here for completeness sake and will undoubtedly be important for some applications in the future, but they are not required for implementing the basic learning systems described in this book.

The first of these enhanced capabilities, and which will be applicable in the very near term, is the ability to gauge the physical location of the user and aspects of the associated environment. Location-aware devices are already becoming prevalent and will clearly become an important aspect of socially aware systems.

Physical Location/Environment

This category includes the *physical location* of a user in absolute terms, but importantly, also the location of the user *relative* to other people or items of interest. This behavioral information may be attained through location-aware mobile devices with Global Positioning System (GPS) or equivalent capabilities, for example. Environment-related information may include, for example, weather conditions. This environmental data may be generated directly from the user's mobile device, or more typically, derivatively from Internet-based sources that can deliver the required information given a user location and the time the user is at the location.

The second of the advanced monitoring categories is a bit more exotic and relates to user physiological information.

Attention/Physiological

Initially this category will focus on behavioral cues such as the direction of the user's gaze, gestures, movements, remarks, et cetera. More exotic future interfaces may enable monitoring physiological responses such as galvanic responses, heart rate, and brain wave patterns. As exotic as this category seems, within a few years these types of behaviors may indeed be an important source of information for at least some types of socially aware system applications (yes, the imagination can run wild!). As just one example of what is in the works, MIT's Media Lab has developed wearable devices that are controlled by gestures.[3] Clearly such interfaces will also be put to use with regard to *interpreting* gestures.

So we have seven categories of behavioral information that socially aware systems can use to facilitate their learning. Note that for all but two of the categories (direct feedback and self-profiling) the behaviors require no separate, explicit action by the user other than just going about her normal business or personal life. So the learning by the socially aware system is basically for "free."

The behavioral categories comprise specific classes of raw behavioral information. Of course, this data, by itself does not make a system socially aware. It is the *patterns* of the behaviors coupled with relevant *inferences* that provide the insights required for social awareness. One dimension of patterns that is invariably important is the *temporal* dimension. Temporal patterns that can provide important insights include the *duration* of a specific behavior, and the specific *sequences* of behaviors over time. For example, the duration of time that a user views a document is likely to be indicative of the level of interest in the document. And, for example, the location of the user over time may provide the system with useful insights that would not be apparent from only being aware of the user's current location.

So most generally, the socially aware system will make inferences on user interests and preferences from patterns of usage behaviors over time. In other words, it will learn from its experience with the user. In fact, it will learn from the *collective* experiences it has with *all* of the user community. This allows the socially aware system to learn faster about any single user than would otherwise be possible because it can detect patterns of similarities *among* users. Where the system finds such correlations among users, it can beneficially bring to bear the larger available body of learning pertaining to a user by applying it to another user for whom less information is available, but who is inferred to be in some aspects similar. (By the way, the general approach of applying the behaviors of others to make inferences on the preferences of a specific person has historically been called "collaborative filtering.")

The socially aware system's inference engine constitutes the heart of the new accelerator of intellectual capital for businesses. The inference engine is a complex set of algorithms that has to glean as many insights as possible from its behavioral knowledge base, while neither under-interpreting nor over-interpreting from this information base. In the next chapter we'll cover some more details on how the inference engine works its magic.

You Own Your Behaviors

But first, we need to take head on *the* key concern that socially aware systems provoke. Undoubtedly, particularly as you read the descriptions of some of the more exotic types of behaviors that can be assessed by a socially aware system, a sort of creepy feeling started to come over you. There is, of course, a very innate, visceral human reaction to being watched or monitored, or just suspecting as much, when you don't expect or much want to be watched or monitored. It's that primeval mammalian response of the hair standing up on the back of the neck that's hardwired into us.

So the natural question on the mind of anyone contemplating socially aware systems is, "What if I don't want my behaviors tracked?" It's the privacy issue. And there is only one viable solution to the issue. You must always be in complete control of tracking and storage of your behavioral information, and it must be *easily* and *transparently* controlled. Socially aware systems must, at a minimum, have two types of controls: first, a very obvious switch that enables you to turn off and turn on at any time the system's capturing of your behavioral information, and second, an ability to *completely* delete your historical behaviors from the system (or equivalently, to make them associated with a user who is completely anonymous to the system). This second function, of course, will delete all the social awareness the system has built up over time with regard to you, but that's your *right*— you should certainly have the ability to invoke this action if desired. Other more fine-grained controls regarding what types of behaviors may be tracked and how the behaviors will be used to make inferences may also be provided, but the overall learning off/on and delete buttons are the mandatory controls.

In addition to control over personal behavioral information, there will undoubtedly also be a curiosity of exactly how the socially aware system is making its inferences. What behavioral information is being used, what is the system deeming relevant and what is not deemed relevant, and what is the logic that is being applied? Some people have been sufficiently concerned about their behavioral history being used in Internet applications that they want to be able to directly inspect their behavioral information that an application has access to at any time. Although at first blush that seems pretty reasonable, the problem is the raw data is going to be incomprehensible to a human without going through a lot of work. And the complexity of the rules and logic of the inference engine are going to be especially inscrutable, even if they were fully available for access, which they are generally not going to be for competitive reasons.

In its most compressed form, your behavioral history ends up being summarized by the socially aware system as a vector or matrix of numbers that represents your unique set of interests and preferences across potentially many thousands of topics and people. Yes, perhaps not the most romantic of notions, but basically you are your vector! In that sense, your interest and preference vector is analogous to your genetic profile. And just as in the case of your DNA, it can be quite fascinating to view your interest vector, to try to discern its patterns, to do some introspection to try to confirm or disconfirm the relative weightings, and perhaps to compare your vector to the vectors of others. But just as in the case of your genetic profile, examining the vector itself only provides you snippets of what the system takes (or "makes" in the case of DNA) to be the "real you." You cannot possibly divine all the patterns that the system can perceive and learn from across the myriad of your vector's values, not to mention the patterns arising from the changes to your vector over time, and finally, on top of all that, the endless mosaics that result from the combinatorial glory of mapping your vector to those of others in innumerable, ingenious ways.

But there is another way to fulfill this desire for more insight into what behavioral information is being used by the system and what inferences are being made from this information, while actually delivering some strong collateral benefits to the user to boot. The *practical* solution to the transparency of how and on what basis the socially aware system is making its inferences is to have the system actually explain itself! That is, the system should provide at least a compressed glimpse of the inference engine's train of thought and the information used to arrive at the system's conclusions and decisions. We'll explore how it can do exactly that in the next chapter.

6

Adaptive Recommendations

A socially aware system has the capability for adapting its interactions and responses to the user in a way that is informed by its learning from behaviors. A very general approach to applying this learning is for the system to deliver *recommendations* to the user. A computer-based recommendation has historically often been narrowly construed to be a suggestion a system makes to a user *without a prompting* by the user. But we will use a broader, and what I think is more practically useful, definition of a system-based recommendation in this book:

> *A recommendation is a suggestion generated by a system that is based at least in part on learning from usage behaviors.*

In other words, a recommendation is an *adaptive* communication from the system to the user. We can be very precise by calling such a recommendation an "adaptive recommendation," but in practice just about all system communications that would be considered recommendations will, in fact, be adaptive recommendations, so I will often drop the "adaptive" modifier in this book.

An advantage of this broader definition is that it enables us to see clearly that other familiar forms of communication from a system to a user are increasingly best understood as just particular forms of (adaptive) recommendations. In particular, an adaptive recommendation may indeed take the form of an unprompted suggestion from the system to a user.

But it may also be a behavioral-based communication back to the user based on at least some degree of *prompting* by the user. A good example is the response to a search request where the response is influenced by search history or other behavioral cues. This is a form of recommendation in which the user reveals more *intentionality* to the system by way of the user providing a phrase to be searched for than is the case for most other types of recommendations. But if the system's response is influenced by behavioral information, then the search result is a form of (adaptive) recommendation by our definition.

By the way, the results generated by modern Internet search engines are in practice *almost always* adaptive recommendations because they are influenced by behavioral information—at a minimum they use the behavioral information associated with people making links from one web page to another. This capability was the original technical breakthrough applied by Google that enabled their search engine to be so much more effective than that of their early competitors.

This feature of contemporary Internet-based search also provides a hint at the reason that the users of enterprise search whom I have talked with over the years have been so often underwhelmed by the performance of their internal searches compared with corresponding Internet versions. Historically, there has been little to no behavioral information embodied within the stored knowledge base of the enterprise, and so search inside the four walls of the business has been basically relegated to the sophisticated, but nonsocially aware, pattern matching of text—similar to the way Internet search was before Google. Without social awareness, search can be a bit of a dud.

Just as Internet search has evolved to become increasingly socially aware, online advertising is inevitably evolving to become more targeted, often using behavioral information to aid in effectively targeting the right advertisement for the right recipient. These types of more intelligently targeted advertisements are also clearly best thought of as just a particular type of recommendation—the only thing that distinguishes them from any other form of recommendation is that they happen to be specially sponsored.

So whether systems are focused on search, advertising, or unprompted recommendations, all are part of a convergence toward the socially aware model of systems, in which the system learns from its experience with its user community and then delivers the learning back to users in one or more of these various forms of adaptive recommendations (figure 6.1). They're systems that have "mirror neurons" and know how to use them!

There are a couple of other things to consider about our definition of recommendations. The "based *at least in part* on learning from usage behaviors" portion of the definition connotes that the system may make use of other information besides behavioral information in generating a recommendation. The nonbehavioral information that may be considered by the system will typically relate to the *contents* of recommended information and/or the *context* of the recommended information. Aspects of the content that could be important in generating a recommendation could include the frequency or position of words or phrases within a document, for example. Contextual attributes that might influence the generation of a recommendation could include

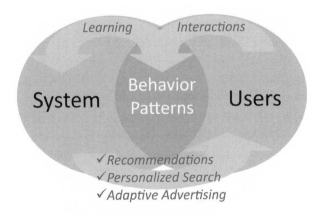

Figure 6.1   Socially Aware Systems in Action

information about the content, such as how recently the document was updated; the form of the document; the author, and so on.

Another noteworthy aspect of our recommendation definition is the "learning from usage behaviors" phrase. Importantly, note that it does not more restrictively read "learning from the usage behaviors of the *recommendation recipient.*" That is because the system may indeed learn from your behaviors in determining a recommendation to deliver to you, but it may instead, or in addition, learn on the basis of the behaviors of *other* users.

A Mind at Work

Now that we have a robust definition of a recommendation, let's delve a little more deeply into the mind of the socially aware system and the way recommendations are actually generated. The process always starts with an understanding of the navigational context of the user. This navigational context can run the gamut from *no* context whatsoever (i.e., the recommendation recipient may not be currently using the system), to a very specific context such as in the case where the user is currently viewing a particular document or has entered a specific term for which the system is to conduct a search.

Given this navigational context, the system needs to choose from a pool of candidate items (i.e., knowledge assets) that could potentially be recommended. So the next step is to evaluate this pool of items against relevant behavioral information, associated patterns, and resulting inferences. This is where the real "AI" part of the system comes into play, and it can be a very complex process indeed, and is beyond the scope of this book to cover in detail. But the following sketch will give you a feel of the basics of the approach.

In the last chapter, we described and categorized the types of behavioral information on which the socially aware system could base its inferences of the interests and preferences of the recommendation recipient. When it comes to making such inferences, this behavioral information is not all created equal! For example, a reference-type behavior, say, where the user *saves* a document for later access, is typically going to be a much more powerful influence on the generation of an inference than if the user just *views* the document. So everything being equal, the inference engine will place more weight on individual reference-type behaviors than pure navigation behaviors. In general, behaviors in which the user has to make some sort of extra effort are more indicative of underlying preferences and interests than actions that require little or no extra effort. Storing items for later reference takes a little extra effort, as does, for example, referring items to others or searching for something. Actions such as contributing content, making a purchase, communicating with another person all take even more extra effort or commitment; so the system will place even more weight on these types of behaviors.

Of course, actions that take extra effort are almost always conducted less frequently than very-easy-to-perform actions such as navigating. So there are invariably going to be relatively more of the individually less informative behaviors for the system to work with. But even if any *one* of these behavioral cues is not highly informative of preferences and interests, *patterns* may emerge that enable the system to make more confident inferences from these types of behaviors. In general, the system has to find the right balance in making inferences from fairly infrequent, but more revealing behaviors, and a larger set of less individually revealing behaviors. Where the inferences from these different types of information align, the system will be pretty confident about its inferences. When they do not, the inference engine has to try to wring some more insight from the data by analyzing it in different ways. If there simply is insufficient data, the system may have to indicate to the user that there is not yet enough of a base of information for the system to provide a recommendation.

The inference engine has to be concerned with, and cognizant of, behavioral patterns *over time*, too, of course. People's interests change with time, and so the inference engine needs to try to tease out long-standing interests from those that come and go as short-term personal and work demands of the user wax and wane.

Given the context, and an inference of a person's preferences and interests, the system then has to decide *whether* to provide a recommendation, and if so, *what* the recommendation will be. Whether to provide a recommendation at all will be a function of the information available for the system to work from. For some contexts, even if there is not yet any relevant behavioral information with which to work, there may be default recommendations that can be confidently made. For example, in a search request, even if there is no usable behavioral information to apply, the system can always default to just relying on the straight matching of the term being searched for with the contents of candidate content. Or if there is no behavioral history at all associated with the person who will receive the recommendation, but there *is* information on content that others have found particularly useful within the same context as that of the recommendation recipient, then that content could be recommended. In practice, although there may be certain situations in which the lack of context or data would force the system to not provide a recommendation, these will be quite rare.

Assuming then, that a recommendation *is* to be delivered, the system will have choices to make on the basis of the interest and preference inferences it has made. It has to match candidate items it is considering recommending with these preferences and interests, and find the best fit given the context. The context is clearly important because it is indicative of what is currently top of mind of the user, whether she is, for example, searching for something, viewing a document, listening to music, or not currently using the system at all. The system needs to also take some other factors into account. For example, is the user already very familiar with a candidate item? If so, there is generally no sense in recommending the item (except in special recommendation cases such as advertising). *Attributes* with regard to a candidate item may also influence the recommendation decision. Is the item recently published? How *influential* is the author? (We will cover how author influence can actually be determined by the system later in the book.) And, of course, what other people thought of the content will be a critical consideration, particularly people whose inferred preference profiles are similar to that of the recommendation recipient.

Tuning and Experimenting

On top of all of this, the user may be provided with some ability to *tune* her recommendations. For example, perhaps the user prefers very recent information at the expense of other characteristics. Or she may wish to place more emphasis on information that is currently particularly "hot" within the community—that is, its popularity is growing quickly. Or perhaps she wants her recommendations to be very highly tuned toward what the system infers is aligned most closely with *her interests*, regardless of other factors such as freshness, quality, and popularity.

These tuning examples are just a few of many other possible recommendation control "dials," but they are representative of three general tuning dimensions that the system will apply regardless of direct user input on the tuning. The first dimension is the degree to which the recommendation will be centered on what the system infers about the *preferences* of the *user*. This could be thought of as the level of egocentrism applied (or desired). The second dimension is the degree of influence the system's inferences about the preferences of other people will have on the recommendation. This can be thought of as how much weight will be given to *social intelligence*. And the third dimension is the degree to which the recommendation will be informed by specific *characteristics* of the *recommended item*. The relative weighting of these dimensions may vary by context or person. For example, if the system has relatively little experience with a user, the social intelligence dimension will undoubtedly be given more weight. Where more intentionality is conveyed by the user, for example, by providing the system with a search term, then clearly the characteristics of potentially recommended items will be the dominant dimension.

Notwithstanding these tuning considerations, alignment with perceived user interests will always be of paramount concern of the system's recommendation function. But the wise system will also sometimes take the user a bit off of her well-worn paths. Think of it as the system running little experiments. Only by "taking a jump" with some of these types of experimental recommendations every now and then can the system fine-tune its understanding of the user and get a feel for potential changes in tastes and preferences. The objective of every interaction of the socially aware system is to find the right balance of *providing* valuable learning to the user in the present, while also interacting so as to *learn more about* the user in order to become even more useful in the future. It takes a deft touch.

A Mind Revealed

The sublime delight of a system that truly surprises with nuggets of insight comes from the complex threads of inferences the system can make. For example, the system can follow long chains of inference such as inferring the fit of a candidate book to recommend to a user based, in part, on the behavioral information generated by *other* people with regard to *other* books by the *same author*, where these other people are individuals in the community of users that the system infers have *similar interests* to the potential recommendation recipient in *specific topical areas*. These derivative chains of logic can be quite complex indeed!

The chains of insight are also a source of fascination, and presented in a summary form to the recommendation recipient can provide a glimpse into the mind of the inference engine, which can be as valuable as the recommendation itself. In other words, the socially aware system can deliver value to the user not just by delivering the "what"— the recommended item—but also by delivering the "why"— the thought process as to how the system arrived at the conclusion that the user would benefit from being aware of, or taking a suggested action with respect to, a specific item or person.

Explanations of recommendations are best delivered by the system in narrative form, just as we would explain a recommendation that we make to a friend. The balance for the socially aware system is to provide enough information to deliver insights that reinforce the credibility of its recommendation, while not overwhelming the recipient with minutia. A truly effective recommendation explanation will not just include the reasons the system thinks the user will benefit from viewing or listening to the recommendation, but also articulate any *reservations* or *doubts* the system has about making the recommendation. For example, the system may be making the recommendation on the basis of limited familiarity with the user's interests, so it may not have a lot of confidence in the recommendation—if so, this would be good for the user to know. Or perhaps the recommendation engine, as it should sometimes do, takes the user off her beaten path of interests and provides a recommendation that is a bit more speculative. That motivation, of course, should be explained to her along with the recommendation (call this a system-to-person change management process!).

As mentioned previously, advertising that is targeted at a recipient on the basis of behavioral information should be considered a form of adaptive recommendation. This form of advertising will clearly supersede the "dumb," socially unaware advertising of the past. Leading media executives, including sage media mogul Barry Diller, have increasingly and emphatically been making the point that behavioral-based advertising that is integrated with content is online advertising's future.[1] As this form of advertising becomes more prevalent, we can expect *explanatory-based advertising* will ultimately become a dominant form. It is inevitable that it will come to be dominant because the recipient understanding the rationale for receiving an advertisement has strong benefits for both the sponsor and the recipient. First, the advertisement has more *credibility* when it is coupled with a good reason of why the recipient should be interested. Second, and a bit more subtly, the transparency of providing a rationale for why the recipient received the ad promotes a greater level of *trust.* Credibility and trust—these are the same factors that are so important in human-based consultative selling, and it is no different for system-based selling!

A Mind Extended

And while on the subject of credibility and trust, there is a related and important idea born of the Web 2.0 era regarding the power of people having *conversations* rather than just consuming broadcasted information, whether broadcasted in traditional publication format or in the form of advertising. Conversations among readers, customers, and other interested parties can be much more meaningful and credible than sponsored, broadcasted information. There is no doubt that conversational media has indeed been an important advance enabled by Web 2.0-based forums. But with the rise of the era of adaptive recommendations, in which the coupled explanations become increasingly interactive and engaging, it is also clear that the term "conversational media" of the future will no longer imply conversations solely among people!

In fact, come climb with me another level or two up the sheer face of abstraction on the subject for a moment. Whether in the form of unprompted suggestions, in the form of responses to requests such as search, or in the form of an advertisement, I don't think it an overstatement that adaptive recommendations and their explanations actually constitute a fundamentally new mode of human communications.

Most of our modes of communications are either one-to-one, such as a telephone call, an instant message, or a private e-mail, or one-to-many, such as a blog, a broadcast e-mail, or a book. Note that what these types of communications have in common is that an *individual* transmits information to one or more other individuals. Even in the case of a collaboratively developed publication, the individual units of communication are from one person, or at most a few collaborators, who generate a unified point of view.

But there are a few types of communication modes that are fundamentally different—these are modes in which the *many* communicate concurrently, but not necessarily collaboratively, to the one or more. They are relatively rare, but have been of utmost importance in the advance of human civilization. The first example of this type of communication is *voting,* in which we do our talking through the ballot box. The preferences of the many are *aggregated* to form a consensus preference that informs the future actions of the group as a whole. This is a pretty simple form of many-to-one communication from an aggregation standpoint—votes are typically just tallied up in a non-weighted manner. A much more sophisticated form of many-to-one communication of preferences is the *market.* Here we "vote" with our money, but the aggregation is much more complex than that of the ballot box—it is iterative and adaptive in nature, resulting in a price that dynamically balances the preferences of all of the market participants and serves to coordinate their activities. Adam Smith's invisible hand is at its core a communications system—the most sophisticated many-to-one communication system the world has ever known.

But now it seems that there is a third fundamental mode of many-to-one communication emerging—our adaptive recommendation. The collective interests and preferences are aggregated through the application of the inference engine to inform the individual. Like the market, and unlike voting, it is an adaptively dynamic process, continuously adjusting as new streams of information become available. But unlike prices, courtesy of the inference engine, the adaptive recommendations come tailored to the individual and with an explanation!

So with the rise of socially aware systems, adaptive recommendations will surely become ubiquitous, and the accompanying explanations will become ever more detailed, nuanced, and interactive. It will be a dramatically different world than the past 50 years of computing. The system will finally become truly worthy of being called a companion or mentor. It's all completely technically feasible and therefore inevitable. But as amazing as that prospect is, it is not nearly the end of the story. We are not done with our recommendation engine. Not by a long shot. We are going to put it to work in a very nonobvious way. And the result of that is going to be of a nature the likes of which we have never before seen.

7

The Learning Layer Emerges

We have seen that the fundamental architecture of learning is the fuzzy network. And we have also seen that we can build systems that pay detailed attention to our behaviors and thereby have a responsive social awareness, where that responsiveness can be manifested as adaptive recommendations and explanations. When we put these two aspects together, we have potentially very powerful learning systems. We actually get much more than that. We get the holy grail of software—systems that literally beneficially *evolve* to become more and more useful.

The trick to creating an automatically evolving system is to apply the preference inferencing capabilities of the socially aware system to generate not just adaptive recommendations for users of the system, but to perform some programming judo and direct recommendations *back onto the system itself*. In other words, enable the system to update the system's own *structure* on the basis of sophisticated inferences from behaviors. And if the system structure is in the form of a fuzzy network, that means the "recommendations" that will be applied will be in the form of suggestions to automatically add or delete nodes, or more typically, to change the weightings of the relationships among the nodes.

These recommendations that are bent back onto the system will therefore be different in form than the ones that are delivered directly to us, but they will similarly be based on inferences from our collective behaviors. In addition to being informed by behavioral information, however, these self-suggestions will also be informed by global considerations with regard to optimum network structure, striving to maintain a proper balance and density of the network.

With this bit of recommendations-in-reverse sorcery we set in motion a very exciting dynamic. The system makes inferences from historical behaviors of users. Then those inferences are applied to automatically modify the structure of the system. This influences the way people use the system, leading to the generation of a new set of behavioral information influenced at least to some degree by the modified system structure. This new behavioral information is included in the overall behavioral history, updated inferences are generated, and the system is again modified accordingly. The process continues indefinitely, resulting in a *coevolving learning network* of inextricably connected people and systems (figure 7.1)!

Our recommendations-in-reverse maneuver is an example of the power of *recursion*. Along with simple but extensible building blocks, such as those that make up our fuzzy network, recursion is often at the heart of systems that project an aura of elegance—systems that exhibit a profound symmetry, and hence beauty, both in their design and their results. Systems built on recursion seem highly compact, yet

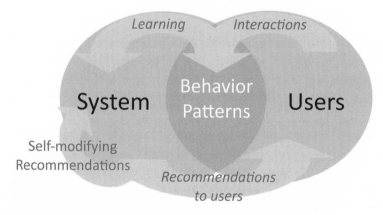

Figure 7.1 Evolving Network of Learning

at the same time powerful in their capabilities, and putting them into motion often results in phenomena with properties that are *emergent*—somehow the whole becomes much greater, and qualitatively different, than the sum of the parts.

Our application of this recursive feedback loop echoes what we discussed with regard to how the brain learns. The brain is a fuzzy network that learns from experience by modifying its connections. But the learning dynamic at work is much richer than that. Some parts of the brain make inferences from external experience, and then make something equivalent to a recommendation to other parts of the brain, causing physical modifications to the brain network. This modification then changes the way future experiences are processed. Just as in the case of our evolving system, this recursive aspect endows the brain its learning power, as well as its wonderful emergent properties—namely a *mind*, replete with complexity, plasticity, creativity, and unpredictability, and embodying a unique personality that evolves over time.

A "Wow" for the Enterprise

Now besides being exceedingly elegant in concept, one of the very practical things this evolving learning network capability means for organizations is that the system can literally *maintain itself*, which implies significantly reduced costs and consistently better user experiences. The system itself will take care of reconfiguring the network to ensure the right content is most easily accessible to the right person at the right time. It will also take care of that annoying, and usually indefinitely postponed, administrative task of archiving content, and do so with a more deft touch than is practically possible manually. The adaptive system will ensure that less useful content will just *fade* into the background of the learning network over time. Contrast this to applying the blunt instrument of manual archiving, where the content ends up being either accessible or not. The learning network that adapts itself on a continuous basis presents us with an ever-unfolding visage colored in nuanced shades rather than black and white.

When we first showed off this type of capability to a small group of IT executives and experts in a very technically sophisticated organization, I received, in one utterance, the feedback that confirmed for me this capability was the "big one" for enterprises.

A group had huddled around a colleague and me in a cramped room at the client site as we ran through the features of our system. Sitting behind me was the senior IT architect for this organization. He was a no-nonsense veteran who had seen and heard just about everything over the course of a 25-plus-year IT career. I could very readily identify with him because I've been on the other side of the table, in his position, having in my CIO days sat through numerous gee-whiz, over-hyped technology presentations. Invariably such sessions end up being either grand, and ultimately unfulfilled, promises or just yawners, so you tend to be pretty jaded going in.

Anyway, while his younger colleagues peppered us with questions, he had been fairly quiet throughout our presentation. But when I described in detail this auto-maintaining capability and showed some actual examples, I heard this barely audible and seemingly involuntary "wow" emanating from behind me. I remember thinking right after the meeting that it was the sound a 12-year-old boy might make when Gisele Bundchen strolls by. He had totally grasped the implications.

Let there be Learning

An especially nice thing about the evolving, self-maintaining learning network concept for large organizations is that it can be implemented in an incremental fashion, and in a manner that complements rather than competes with existing systems. Specifically, the learning network can in effect be a true learning *layer* that rests on top of existing systems and content. The learning layer can be very "thin"—in a minimal implementation it can just consist of an unobtrusive web of relationships that are created among the existing systems and content, along with usage behaviors captured by the learning system, and of course, the inference engine and recommendation generating capabilities of the learning system. This incremental and complementary approach to implementation is very different than enterprises have become used to with regard to with applications such as enterprise resource planning and content management systems, for example. Traditionally, such applications have required a *replacement* of existing systems, leading to scary, irrevocable implementation decisions and large-scale and long-lasting disruptions for users. Implementation of a learning layer has exactly the opposite characteristics.

A typical initial implementation of a learning layer starts with identifying existing systems and content to be included in the learning network. The learning network treats all computer-based resources in a uniform way whether they are web pages, documents, multimedia, or computer applications. In practice, a very light weight "wrapper" is established for each resource to turn it into a "content object," or most broadly a "knowledge asset." The process of identifying resources to include in the learning layer may be facilitated by search engines.

A set of appropriate topical areas associated with the learning network can then be established. Next, relationships are established among the existing resources and the learning layer's topics, as well as among the knowledge assets themselves as desired. Again, some enterprise search engines can be applied to facilitate this process by generating a set of first-cut relationships. All of this can be done *virtually* by simply creating linkages to existing content—no physical copying of information is necessitated.

What we have done so far is to basically prime the pump. Once the learning network is established, it begins to adapt as soon as people begin using it. Very quickly it builds up

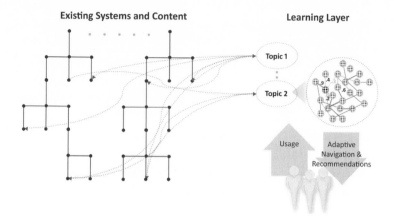

Figure 7.2 Bootstrapping a Layer of Learning

sufficient information to infer preferences and interests and to start delivering useful recommendations to users. Shortly thereafter, the learning layer has sufficient information to make inferences on useful self-modifications to its network, and will begin adapting its structure (figure 7.2). As users continue to interact with the learning layer, the pace of the learning accelerates, and the integrated system-user network becomes more and more productive. It's scalable learning in action.

We saw that adaptive recommendations, in any of their various forms, are a key means for the socially aware system to deliver learning back to its users. But the learning layer can deliver even more than just specific recommendations to us. It can potentially deliver an entire *user interface* that automatically adapts! What each person sees (or hears) that is generated by the network can be driven by collective learning. Specific organizations can have easy access to the information most relevant to its members. The form of the interface can be varied—3-D navigation that allows a user to "fly" through the universe of the learning network is just one obvious example. And the beauty of all of this is that it is *free*—the learning layer automatically generates and adapts these interfaces—it does not require an IT department to set up a complex set of individual sites or web pages.

The learning layer always adheres to the underlying security of the information referenced by its knowledge assets. So that comes free as well. Additional permission structures within the learning layer itself can be easily set and managed by the users of the network. People simply own their own creations, and then can extend various levels of permissions to others as they desire. The adaptive recommendations and user interface and all other functions of the learning layer automatically understand and obey these permissions. The entire learning layer truly self-regulates and manages itself!

More than Just Us

In the Introduction, I made the claim that adaptation based on experience constitutes the third major wave in the evolution of IT. These IT waves are heavily influenced by an underlying driver of the evolution of computing—over long periods of time software can be seen to inevitably evolve through increasing *levels of abstraction*. What that means is that layers of technology build on underlying layers that are lower level, or in other words, that are further removed from the level of every day human experience. For example, once upon a time people had to program everything themselves to get a computer to do much of anything for them. Then operating systems became available that automatically took care of a lot of the administrative things, and a visual metaphor of a desktop became standard. This was followed by the availability of various general purpose applications that ran on top of the operating system. Then applications specific to business purposes developed. Software evolves this way because people ultimately want to perform a task at hand on *their* terms, not learn to use a system on *its* terms. The IT industry strives to ultimately build systems that people can deal with on the same terms as they do with each other. Yet, each technical advance has to be built on layers below.

The learning layer is just a continuation of this inevitable evolutionary phenomenon of computing. It is a software layer that is in a sense "higher level" than the underlying systems on which it rests, because it more effectively and directly interacts with people on their terms. But it is also backward compatible with the system layers below. In fact, the learning layer is a "force multiplier"—it actually amplifies the value of these underlying layers.

While built on other systems, and amplifying those system levels below, the learning layer is of a fundamentally different *nature*. It is the next level of systems abstraction, and that alone brings benefits, just as previous steps up the ladder of abstraction have brought us benefits. But in addition to this jump in abstraction, its recursive nature promises *emergent* properties—epiphenomenal properties, as philosophers would put it. Yes, the learning layer can more directly interact with people on their own terms. But there is more. It is only a bunch of relationships, behaviors, and inferences. It is just a system. And yet it learns. It *evolves*. It is not just an "it"—it is *us*—and yet *more* than just us.

8

Social Networks and Knowledge Management Unite!

By now most of us have some familiarity with social networks, with Facebook and LinkedIn being some current leading examples. They are arguably the most powerful trend in Internet applications of the past few years. In fact, in many ways social networks were really the first *fundamentally* new class of application that was a direct result of, and could only exist in their present form because of, the shift in the center of gravity of computing structures from hierarchies to networks. It seems quite quaint in today's world of ubiquitous networks of friends and colleagues to remember back that only a little more than a decade ago the people-based structure most of us were best acquainted with was the venerable hierarchical organization chart.

Not surprisingly given their popularity in facilitating our personal lives, many businesses have been at least experimenting with social network systems inside their organization. These same businesses have generally had a long experience using content management systems to manage their documents. So why are these two types of systems separate?

The answer is there is no reason they need to be or should be—it is just historical accident that content management came first and was oriented from the beginning toward larger organizations. And because of this earlier inception of content management systems, unlike social networks, they were born of a time before the network paradigm had come to the fore. So they were based squarely on the hierarchy. The social network systems that developed later were not only firmly rooted in the network paradigm, they were also initially oriented toward individuals, for whom content management was generally a secondary concern at best. So content management and social networks have been disconnected in their timing, structures, and target user segments.

In fact, in some companies there remains a bit of a stigma with regard to social networks because of their roots in the teenager and young adult demographic, and even due to perhaps an undertone of an association with sites oriented toward flirting and dating. As an example of this phenomenon, I was recently talking with executives at a well-known international technology and engineering firm about managing enterprise knowledge, and they indicated that internally they did not use the term "social networks," but rather, were careful to call them "*expertise* networks." This was precisely because of the less than serious connotations that were associated with social networks in some quarters of the company!

Regardless of how we choose to label it, going forward it is clearly an imperative for businesses that the operations and management of their social networks and their content are fully integrated. Intellectual capital comes in two forms—that which resides solely in the minds of people (sometimes referred to as *tacit* knowledge in the vernacular of KM), and that which is embodied in documents and systems (sometimes referred to as *explicit* knowledge). Integrating social networks and content management therefore enables the integrated management of enterprise intellectual capital. And it is pretty hard to have the real advantages you are striving for with regard to learning to learn better without this integration.

The Fuzzy Union

The good news is that our architecture of learning, the fuzzy network, naturally handles this integration. People clearly comprise networks, and the relationships between people are not necessarily just digital in nature. We all have some relationships that are very strong, and others that are much weaker. Some people are our soul mates, some are friends, some are colleagues, and some are just acquaintances. There are shades of gray in our social relationships, just as in the case of relationships among items of content and topics. And there are different *types* of relationships among people, and among people and content that should be explicitly recognized. Some of these types of relationship may, in fact, *be* digital—for example, someone is your classmate or is not; someone is an author of an item of content or is not. But some types of relationships, such as the degree of similarity of preferences between two people, or the degree of interest a person or a group of people have with regard to a topical area, clearly will not be digital. They will be much more nuanced than that.

Our fuzzy network-based learning layer can treat representations of people (in their most basic form we can call these representations simply "profiles") in the same manner as content-based objects. As such, these people "objects" can be connected to other people objects and relevant content objects. This extensibility of the learning network to handle content and people so similarly is what enables the learning layer to so powerfully intertwine an organization's people and knowledge assets. The value generated by integrating people and knowledge assets into a single learning network is much greater than the sum of the values of separate content and social network systems.

For example, the degree of similarity of interests and preferences of people can be more effectively assessed in this integrated learning network than in a stand-alone social network as a consequence of the system being able to correlate people's relative levels of interests with regard to various topics and content within the learning network. And expertise can be more finely and credibly assessed in the learning network than by just relying on the self-profiling of self-proclaimed experts that is so common in first generation social networks. For instance, the inference engine of the learning layer can map the knowledge contributions of people to the network to very finely grained topical areas, and thereby gain a much more detailed perspective into the perceived value of the contributions to specific cohorts of users. This enables the learning layer to attain far deeper insights into which person might currently be of the most value to another person in the network within a particular context than is possible with just a standalone social network.

Integrating representations of people with knowledge assets supercharges the evolving learning network concept. It enables the learning layer to work with an even greater set of behaviors, and to deliver a richer, more finely tuned, array of recommendations, including recommendations of people. It allows the learning layer to get a much sharper picture of the real *you*, along with everyone else in the learning network. Yes—you may be just a vector of numbers, but what a huge, ever-changing, finely tuned, nuanced, and endlessly patterned vector of numbers you are!

The Power of People Recommendations

The capability of the socially aware system to effectively recommend *people* to other people represents a particularly significant advantage for larger organizations. The reality is that much of an organization's knowledge, even within organizations with a strong documentation ethic, remains tacit. So enabling on-the-mark suggestions of people with the particular expertise that can enhance the efforts of others is a productivity imperative.

The integrated learning layer that intertwines people and knowledge assets serves to overcome some of the limitations of our native ability to build and maintain social networks.

For example, there is a recognized limit, known as Dunbar's number, with regard to our being able to mentally keep up with our relationships with others—estimated to be on the order of about 150 people (although it has been suggested to me personally that there are those among us who struggle with a small fraction of that number!).[1] Ordinarily that would be about the limit of the network of people from whom we could directly learn in an interactive manner. But the learning layer's ability to augment our native abilities through its continuous efforts on our behalf to discern relevant patterns and connections, bringing the right people and their content to our attention when they are most needed, overcomes the Dunbar limit many times over. Our learning is unshackled from the old bounds.

Recommendations of people to other people will typically be driven by one of two types of inferences by the system: a matching of a perceived *need* for expertise of one party with an inferred *appropriate level* of expertise of another party, or a matching of two parties that have an inferred *similar* set of interests or expertise. Both of these types of recommendations can be important for building additional learning into the fabric of an organization.

The first type, the matching of expertise *demand* with bona fide expertise *supply* is the more obviously valuable one. Left to its own devices, learning languishes in organizational islands. The learning layer overcomes that tendency with its adaptive recommendations, establishing flows of learning that serve to institutionalize a collective apprenticeship capability. Such learning within the context of daily work activities can be a powerful and indispensable supplement to formalized training. So this type of people recommendation serves to accelerate the *transfer* of learning to those in the organization with relatively less expertise in a given area.

But the second basis of people recommendations, in which *similarity and depth of interests* is inferred is also of great importance. In this case, the learning layer encourages people with strong interests to *amplify* those interests by connecting and collaborating with other people that together have the passion, energy and expertise to deepen their common knowledge base and then contribute this deeper knowledge to the learning layer. Whereas the first type of people recommendation provides a basis for getting members of an organization to *common levels* of expertise, this second type of recommendation promotes discovery and innovation to get the organization to the *next level* of expertise in a given area.

These two bases for people recommendations correspond nicely to two classes of organizational knowledge that the authors of the *Mobilizing Minds* distinguish: an organization's *proprietary* knowledge and its *distinctive* knowledge.[2] Proprietary knowledge is required to maintain competitiveness, and can be applied to get those not already at a threshold level of expertise "up-to-speed." Distinctive knowledge, on the other hand, represents unique and valuable expertise typically originating from an individual or small group. This is the type of knowledge that can drive competitive advantage. Over time, distinctive knowledge should migrate to become proprietary knowledge.

It is readily seen, then, that recommendations of the *more expert* person to the *less expert* is a way for the learning layer to accelerate the transfer of *proprietary* knowledge throughout the organization. And recommendations of *experts* to other *experts* are a means of accelerating the creation and dissemination of *distinctive* knowledge within the organization. Both are critical in accelerating intellectual capital formation.

High-quality people recommendations delivered by the learning layer also have a subtle but important *psychological* advantage. If a person needs some expert advice or just wants to make contact with another person because of what seem to be common interests, there can often by a bit of reluctance to reach out. We have all experienced this kind of hesitancy and it is at its root driven by a fear of embarrassment of asking for help, or approaching the wrong person, and in the worst case receiving some form of rejection or at least a perception thereof. All it takes is one of those bad experiences to put a long-lasting damper on seeking assistance.

The beauty of credible recommendations of other people made by the learning layer is that it significantly reduces the hesitancy in making connections because the system can take the "blame" if there is any misfire. "The system suggested I contact you," is a very powerful phrase for both of the parties of a people recommendation. For the person *needing* assistance, it provides cover. For the person whose assistance is recommended by the system, if he is not the best fit to address the issue, or simply is too busy to help, he will more likely be able to honestly communicate that back to the person needing help. The embarrassment factor inherent to such communications for both parties is vastly reduced. The system as an intelligent but not necessarily infallible intermediary enables a "no harm, no foul" level of interactions. Together with the learning layer *uncovering* valuable connections that might not otherwise be found, this positive *psychological* aspect of people recommendations promotes a much *healthier flow* of expertise throughout the organization.

Measuring the Flow

In addition to valuable recommendations of people, another benefit of the integrated social and knowledge learning network is the automatic generation of a variety of *metrics* that strongly incentivize collaboration and contributions to the organization's base of knowledge. A very basic example is the popularity metric, which simply keeps track of the number of accesses by other people of knowledge assets contributed by an individual or team. And this type of metric can be assessed across an entire learning network or for specific suborganizations. Other simple metrics include the number of knowledge assets contributed, the number of other knowledge assets that other people have connected to an author's knowledge assets, and the number of referrals of a person or their authored or managed knowledge assets.

An example of a more sophisticated measurement of an individual's or team's learning value-add is *influence*. Influence can come in several forms. The *direct* influence that a particular knowledge contributor has on another person can be calculated on the basis of the extent to which the person has exhibited behavioral patterns indicative of interest in the knowledge contributor's content. For example, accessing a significant number of items of the content of the knowledge contributor, saving some of his content for later reference, referring his content to other people, or especially, making direct contact with the knowledge contributor, would all be indicative of a fairly high level of direct influence. On the other, few or no accesses of the contributor's works would be indicative of low (direct) influence on the particular person. This type of direct influence calculation cuts both ways—if you are a member of a learning network and make contributions to the network, the direct influence you have on other specific people can be calculated, as well as who influences you and to what extent.

Complementary to this type of direct pair-wise influence calculation (in which one or both of the pair can be a *group* rather than just an individual), a more *general* influence metric can also be generated. This metric determines the influence a person has across the entire learning network. To make this calculation the system takes into account the secondary, tertiary, and so on, effects that are ignored by the pair-wise influence metric. That is, it takes into account not only the direct effects of you influencing someone, but also the resulting ripple effect of those people influencing other people, and that set of people influencing yet another set of people, and so on. In other words, it is a recursively generated metric that determines the propagation of influence across the network. The result is then typically normalized to provide a *relative* sense of the influence, and by extension the *value*, of the contribution to learning people have across the entire learning network.

Some readers may be familiar with the hitherto relatively obscure field called social network analysis. It is an analytic technique for examining information flows in an organization. It can provide considerable insights, but historically it has required in-person interviews or survey forms to attain the data required for the analysis. It was time consuming and expensive—and was therefore not applied in most organizations. If it was conducted, it was done very rarely so the results would inevitably go stale with time. But with its ability to generate a variety of meaningful metrics such as influence, and to display the results in a variety of graphical forms, the learning layer solves this problem—it performs a powerful, automatic and continuous social network analysis for free!

Our discussion of influence has centered on the influence of *people*, and this metric will be of keen interest. But the influence of *any* knowledge asset can just as easily be generated and such a metric can also provide valuable insights. In fact, the influences of knowledge assets are calculated by the system anyway to determine the influence of people, since the level of influence of a person is just the sum of the influence of each of the knowledge assets the person has authored or created. As in the case of the general influence of people, the general influence of a knowledge asset is a combination of the influence it exerts on the basis of its inferred *direct* importance to users based on their behaviors, and the *indirect* importance that is a consequence of the propagation of its influence across the web of relationships of the learning network.

So with these metrics we can readily observe the relative influence of individual items of content in addition to the influence of a specific person. For example, we can easily answer questions such as "What is the most influential article or video in the learning network?" or "Who authors the most influential content in a particular topical area?" The answers to these types of questions provide *individuals* the feedback required to tune their knowledge contributions for maximum benefit to the organization, and also suggest to the *organization* appropriate areas for emphasis and reward. And influence provides strong guidance to the learning layer on how it should automatically reshape itself. And again, this power can only be fully achieved through our architecture of learning in which the social network and the learning network are one and the same!

Earlier in the book we wrestled with the concept of learning—it's a pretty abstract term, so we even resorted to some math to try to get a better handle on it. And we concluded that it is a flow. But when the learning layer enables us to actually *see* a display of the influences pulsing through our network, the abstract concept comes alive. We can make learning a visual reality in our organizations and behold our learning *in action*. Learning is the lifeblood of a business, and we can see that lifeblood not only *is* a flow, but *does* flow, and in a measurable way.

9

Processes That Learn

We have seen how our evolving learning layer of integrated social and knowledge networks can accelerate enhancements to an organization's intellectual capital. But as impressive as that opportunity is, it is not the end of the story. Business processes, and the corresponding workflow, can be built to actually adapt on the basis of this same learning infrastructure!

A business process is a disarmingly simple concept—it is just a series of activities that yields a business result. And workflow is a *specific sequence of steps* within the process. These days that all seems obvious enough, but the business process redesign revolution that originated in the early 1990s rested on the simple insight that a business was, in fact, composed of processes—processes often spanning, and quite often obscured by, more traditional organizational boundaries.

Recognition of this simple fact should by itself naturally lead to an emphasis on improving the performance of businesses by improving processes, and to some degree it did. But the concept really gained mainstream momentum driven by two major factors: the belated and somewhat panicked recognition that an emphasis on process-based performance was a key contributor to Japanese manufacturers of the 1980s significantly outperforming their American and European counterparts, and the intellectual leadership of Michael Hammer and his colleagues in evangelizing the concept at a more strategic level. And the result was that process reengineering had a big impact on just about every medium to large organization in the world. As mentioned in the Introduction, process redesign and the leverage of the Internet have clearly been two of the biggest stories behind the business productivity gains of the past 15 years.

By the middle of the 1990s a fairly standard methodology had developed for conducting a process redesign project. The methodology was applied by many different consulting companies, and there were associated variations, but the general approach was pretty similar. Following is a sketch of the basic steps employed.

Traditionally, the first step in improving process performance was to identify the current processes, many of which had not even been formally recognized previously. The second step was to redesign the process as appropriate to improve efficiency and effectiveness. The third step was to determine the infrastructure required to support the redesigned process—and often enhanced IT was a critical part of the required infrastructure. And the fourth step was implementation of the redesigned process and supporting infrastructure. Particularly for transactional-based processes, this process reengineering approach was pretty effective. By debottlenecking and standardizing processes, better process throughput at lower cost was often achieved.

A Forced Fit

However, traditional process redesign generally stalled when there was an attempt to apply it in the non-transactional, knowledge and expertise-intense areas of the business. In those areas, the prescribing of a "one size fits all" workflow up-front yielded processes that were too brittle to accommodate the complexity of the actual work activities. The result for these types of organizations was that they either ended up with formalized processes that actually *decreased* process performance due to lack of flexibility, or they ended up with inefficiencies and highly variable results because they defaulted back to essentially ad hoc approaches.

I've seen both of these unfortunate outcomes firsthand in multiple organizations. I got a good dose of the first type of outcome when I led an early process reengineering effort spanning a multi-billion dollar chemicals enterprise. To support the redesigned processes, we implemented the leading ERP software of the day. All worked fine for the financial transactions-based part of the business, for manufacturing, and for routine sales processes. However, when we tried to apply it to marketing and other "knowledge-intense" parts of the organization, the immune response to both the prescribed processes and the brittle IT system meant to support the redesigned process was intense. We spent most of the project on "change management" matters; change management basically being a euphemism for trying to convince people to embrace something that really just didn't fit their circumstances.

More often these days I encounter the other extreme. At ManyWorlds, we focus most of our advisory services on decision and knowledge-rich organizations such as R&D, strategy and planning, business development, and marketing. In the majority of these organizations there is typically very little in the way of process consistency, much less standardization. For example, in the chemicals project I described above, we didn't even attempt to address R&D. And that is pretty standard for R&D, as well as for other business areas with similar characteristics—they are areas that to this day enterprise process improvement initiatives fear to tread. Of course, the result is that these process areas are prone to widespread inefficiencies and knowledge isolation. And the term "process" itself has become a dirty word in some management circles owing to the bad memories. I've come across a number of executives who now prefer the word "practice" to "process," for example. I suppose the idea is to try to soften the traditional connotations of a rigid sequence of activities and steps.

A Weaving of Work and Learning

But now we have a way to address the process needs of organizations that skipped the first generation of process reengineering, or wish they had. The power of adaptive networks enables a new approach that delivers the advantages of process reengineering, but overcomes the traditional brittleness problem by allowing for the adaptation of workflow to the different requirements of the process participants, and allowing for the process as a whole to automatically adapt over time to changing requirements.

We can make all of this happen by simply once again turning to our architecture of learning, the fuzzy network, and recognizing that we can incorporate process sequences within the network. As you know, a fuzzy network can have many different types of relationships between any two nodes. So we can include a special type of relationship, a *process sequence*, within our network. By doing so, we continue to benefit from all of the power of our integrated social and knowledge learning network, and then additionally benefit from the network tuning itself to support specific business processes.

In other words, as a user traverses a process, the learning layer can automatically adapt to provide the optimal supporting information for the particular process step being executed. And even better, where there are multiple process step options, the learning layer can deliver recommendations on which of the process step options to take. So, for example, a novice may get a recommendation for a different sequence of process steps (e.g., step "3b" in figure 9.1) than an expert (e.g., "3a" in the figure). And, of course, preferably she will receive an explanation of *why* the process step was suggested. Imagine it as a process "cockpit" in which the system helps you do the flying, and the instrumentation panel actually adapts to each specific stage of the flight!

Because the workflow is woven right into the learning layer itself, it also offers the opportunity for "recombinant" processes, where process sections can be cleaved off and

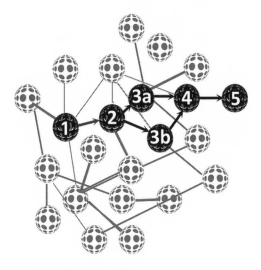

Figure 9.1   Adaptive Process Network

recombined to form new, synthetic processes. This is the ultimate in flexibility and efficiency, and can serve to make the benefits of processes realizable in even the most complex and fluid of work settings. Think of it as basically the means for the *mass customization* of business processes.

So now we have the final piece of a fundamentally new business phenomenon: a learning layer that incorporates not just people and knowledge, but also process. This provides us with all of the levers necessary to generate new levels of business performance. And the learning layer does not need to be, nor should it be, confined to within the four walls of a business—the learning layer can flexibly extend its processes *across* a *network* of organizations. The authors of "The Big Shift" suggest that "[t]he ultimate differentiator among companies, though, may be a competency for creating and sharing knowledge across enterprises."[1] I would go even further and argue that the ability to flexibly create and share *adaptive process networks* across companies will become a driver of performance differentiation. "The network is the business" is a slogan that the learning layer can now make a reality.

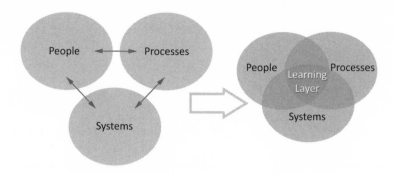

Figure 9.2 The New Synthesis of People, Processes, and Systems

The admonition to pay attention to people, processes, and technology is the centerpiece of many modern enterprise performance improvement initiatives. And although it has become a bit of a cliché over the years, it nevertheless remains valid. The learning layer gives the tired old phrase some new life, however. If we tweak the term "technology" a bit, and substitute the term "systems" instead—since it is the *software* level of IT that is most relevant with regard to both people and processes—we see that our learning layer transforms the cliché into an integrated reality. People, processes, and the supporting systems actually *merge* in a behavioral sense at the learning layer (figure 9.2).

You may recall from the Introduction that a limitation that has been identified with the Web 2.0 generation of technology in enterprises was that it rather quickly reached diminishing returns because the tools were not well integrated into people's routine workflow. We have solved that problem here: the learning layer itself *is* the workflow. The daily flow of work and flow of learning become inseparable, as they should be.

PART III

BUILDING LEARNING INTO THE FABRIC OF BUSINESS

10

The Fabric of Business

The wonders of the learning layer lie before us. We want to build learning into the fabric of our businesses and we now have the means to do so. But what do we mean exactly by the *fabric* of business? It sounds catchy—but does it have some real content? Well, yes, it is a metaphor; we employ metaphors to convey concepts that are otherwise tough to directly describe. And with the term "fabric" we want to convey the notion of the very *essence* or *nature* of the business. Something essential, something core, something woven throughout. We can try to itemize some characteristics to add some clarity; certainly, the essential nature of a business must include how it creates value for its customers, its capabilities and core competencies, the way its people interact among themselves and with others, the processes it employs, and its culture and values. We could maybe boil down what we mean by "fabric" to the basic elements of strategy, capabilities, and culture, where capabilities most broadly considered include assets, processes, and people. Somehow, though, our business fabric seems like it should be more than just the sum of these elements, just as the engaging patterns of a tapestry emerge from the weaving of the different types of threads in particular ways—which, of course, is exactly the point of the choice of the metaphor.

We know that the fabric is going to somehow have a different feel for different businesses, and to some extent, different even across organizations within a business. So we need a way to get a measure of our cloth—a way to establish its metes and bounds, as well as its texture. Let's see if we can do so by starting with some first principles. The most basic thing we can be sure of about business is that businesses are *in business* to create value. So a fundamental aspect of our fabric must be the business's model for generating value. We could call this the company's strategy, its business model, its profit model, or just its *raison d'etre*. And we can identify three major extremes in the ways in which value can be generated, which will serve to delimit the boundaries of our business tapestry. These positions are based on a contemporary evolution of earlier business strategy models, and we will cover details and implications in more depth later, but I first want to just very briefly describe these three "pure form" positions.[1]

The first extreme is occupied by those businesses that thrive by producing an indisputably superior product (where the term *product* should be thought of as broadly covering *services* as well). Since product superiority ultimately rests on superior innovation, we will call a business with this *raison d'etre* a "Product Innovator." The second positional extreme that we can identify is that of businesses having truly superior *relationships* with their customers, and in their ultimate form, relationships that become exclusive in nature. We can label a business with this type of model for generating value a "Relationship Owner." And the third extreme is the model of *positioning* to encompass the portion of the network of supply lying between the production of a product and the ultimate customer that generates the greatest value. We will call a business operating under this model a "Supply Network Architect."

So we have now at least established some extremes on which our cloth is draped. It's really pretty simple in concept—you can make money by having the best product or the best relationship with a customer, or by being best positioned within the chain of activities that lie between the production of a product and the delivery of a solution that includes the product to the end consumer.

But here's the thing—businesses operating at these absolute extremes are far and few between. In the sometimes relatively naïve world of strategy development of the past, executives were exhorted to make sure their business was at an extreme position on a strategic framework of one sort or another. Don't get "stuck in the middle" was the familiar refrain from armies of management consultants, with their formidable looking strategy treatises in hand. And dutifully we executives strived to ensure that our business adhered to the characteristics of a pure-form strategic position, even if it felt like a force fit at times. But there is an old adage from the world of boxing that every executive in the midst of brutal competition comes to understand every bit as well as the intrepid soul who ventures into the ring: "Everybody has a strategy until the first time they get hit."

Companies have to be prepared to navigate among strategic positions. If you stay in the same place you will inevitably get hit. Maybe it will be because of disruptive technologies, or perhaps globalization, or changes in the regulatory playing field, or the fickleness of consumers' tastes. Or maybe it will just be because someone else thinks, even if initially misguided, that they can do exactly the same thing as you, only better, or faster, or cheaper. All businesses will eventually catch a punch to the face. And if they stay flat-footed they will get hit again and again. And when they get hit and they need to move they can't just magically *jump* to another strategic position. They have to *travel* to the desired position. As they navigate this migration, the fabric of the business— their competencies, processes, people, and their very culture and values—will have to travel with them, and will need to adapt accordingly. Not completely, of course—there is an essence that remains invariant, the part of the business truly built to last. And as we know full well, a good part of what must be built to last is the learning of the organization.

But if positions change somewhat, and it is inevitable that they will, something has to give. The fabric of the business will need to adapt. In some cases only a bit; in other cases much more dramatically. So sorry again Aristotle, but

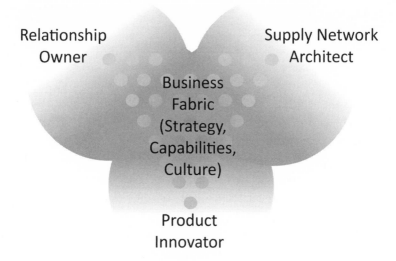

Relationship
Owner

Supply Network
Architect

Business
Fabric
(Strategy,
Capabilities,
Culture)

Product
Innovator

Figure 10.1   The Business Fabric Framework

a business's strategy and the fabric that it wraps itself in is necessarily fuzzy (figure 10.1). Sometimes you can't stay at one of the extremes. Sometimes that is by your choice, and sometimes it is because in the near term you simply have no choice.

Our tapestry appears on the surface to be simple, and yet the deeper you look, the more complexity becomes apparent. A good way to start to get a better understanding of the complex often comes from probing its extremes, so let us investigate a bit more the three positions that serve to delimit the boundaries of our business tapestry.

The Product Innovator position is a good place to begin our more detailed investigations because it is the place where most businesses set off on their commercial journey. This type of business's fundamental competitive differentiation is based on the *attributes* of its products themselves—the business thrives or dies on that basis. To the extent that processes are important to this business model, they are of primary concern in the specific area of product development. The organizational structures of Product Innovators reflect the relative lack of reliance on large-scale processes— these businesses are almost always organized around product lines. This often makes for significant inefficiencies in the various functional areas such as finance, HR, manufacturing, et cetera, because these functions have considerable duplication across the product lines. This inefficiency is tolerated, however, since being as good as possible in product-related areas brings these companies advantages that overwhelm the organizational efficiency disadvantages.

Most businesses start out as Product Innovators because the entrepreneur that launches a business is typically motivated by having a better product idea than what is currently available in the marketplace. We can think of the Product Innovator area of our tapestry as the position of "creative destruction" because it is the most usual initial position from which marketplace incumbents are attacked. Product Innovators attack the incumbents by producing products that are much better in performance and only slightly more expensive, or through the more classically disruptive manner of producing products that are good enough functionally but are much less expensive than current products.

Some businesses can remain successful with this model, and although they may make some adjustments here and there, they may never leave the general realm of the Product Innovator. But other businesses, whether by necessity or design, begin to rely on value-creating points of differentiation versus other marketplace participants on the basis of factors other than the product itself. In general, these non-product factors boil down to *process-related* factors of some type. So the degree to which processes in general serve to differentiate marketplace performance versus competitors is a key dimension of our business model tapestry.

And as process becomes increasingly important, a business has a fundamental choice to make on the primary *orientation* of its process approach. It can choose to focus on building processes and supply chains or networks *toward* customers, or it can choose to start with the customer and then *work backwards*, building processes, and chains or networks of supply, to fulfill customer demands.

The ultimate conclusion of the first approach is our Supply Network Architect position. These are businesses that are able to design and manage processes that extend across not only the enterprise, but also across an overall business network. The most successful of these businesses are able to position themselves within this overall business network in a way that maximizes value capture from the network as a whole. These businesses seek to be in a position in which they *uniquely* fill a valuable area of the network, and work to try to ensure that all other areas of the network are filled with intensely competitive complementary companies. In other words, "one of me, and many of them" is the position these companies strive to achieve and to maintain. Their ultimate objective is to manage the value flow of the business ecosystem around them.

The logical conclusion of the second process orientation approach, the working-backwards-from-the-customer orientation, is our Relationship Owner position. These businesses flourish or flounder on the basis of establishing a relationship with customers that is stronger than that of any competitor. Implicit in this business model position is the assumption that owning the customer relationship is the most important portion of the strategic real estate. Again, in this position, the key to value capture is "one of me, and many of them." The ideal situation is to have exclusive access to the customer, and whereby the suppliers to the Relationship Owner are numerous and in intense competition, thereby reducing their ability to capture value from the Relationship Owner's "demand chain."

Drivers of Value

We can get a sharper focus on the patterns of our tapestry by considering *value drivers*. Value drivers are a business's most important levers of value creation versus their competition. To be successful at our strategic extremes, a business must absolutely be better than their competitors with regard to their core value drivers. As you would expect, our three fundamental business model positions have very different core

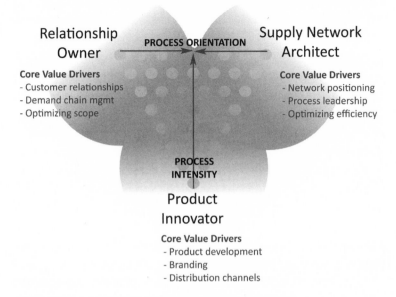

Relationship
Owner

PROCESS ORIENTATION

Supply Network
Architect

Core Value Drivers
- Customer relationships
- Demand chain mgmt
- Optimizing scope

Core Value Drivers
- Network positioning
- Process leadership
- Optimizing efficiency

PROCESS
INTENSITY

Product
Innovator

Core Value Drivers
- Product development
- Branding
- Distribution channels

Figure 10.2   Value Drivers of the Business Fabric

value drivers due to their maximal distance on our tapestry from one another. And three core value drivers stand out for each of our three business model extremes (figure 10.2).

The Product Innovator model is characterized by the core value drivers of product development, branding, and distribution channels. First among equals is product development—this model can only generate value if the product itself is superior, and product superiority is a function of the product development *process*. Branding is extraordinarily important to the Product Innovator as it represents the "information bundle" that is created in the mind of the customer that embodies the business's product superiority. And access to strong or privileged distribution channels is critical as the Product Innovator requires an effective way to deliver its product to its customers, since it is not the customer relationship or distribution channel owner.

The classic example of the Product Innovator is 3M; Apple is another iconic example. Relatively young industries such as the biotech and cleantech industries are predominantly populated by Product Innovator companies. The fabric of this type of business includes the sustained cultivation of deep competencies and capabilities that contribute to competitive advantages of their products. In the case of 3M, for example, it is sustaining the world's broadest and deepest knowledge of adhesives. For Apple it is the capability for elegance of design of integrated software and hardware solutions that result in superior user experiences. When you walk through the halls of a true Product Innovator, you can't help but notice that you are in the midst of a culture infused with creativity, an environment in which people are often encouraged to spend a good deal of unstructured time in the pursuit of new ideas, and in which you will be invited insistently into their offices (or more likely, open work spaces) so that they might share their ideas and creations with you.

The Supply Network Architect has a very different set of core value drivers, namely network positioning, process leadership, and optimizing efficiency. Network positioning is the most critical element of value creation and capture for these companies—being in the right place in the network versus in the wrong place in the network can be worth literally orders of magnitude of value. Think of Microsoft versus Gateway, for example, in the personal computer supply network of the 1990s, or Wal-Mart in the retail space. And these businesses do not leave their positioning to happenstance. They are continuously adjusting their position, and when possible, the position of others in the ecosystem, to their advantage.

These businesses also need to demonstrate leadership or best practices in at least a few process areas. The key is to be focused on leadership in the process areas that create the greatest value given the circumstances. For example, Cisco Systems has historically had sustained process advantages in marketing and acquisitions that led to superior performance versus its competition. And a general focus on optimizing for efficiency is critical for companies in this position. Standardization and the application of scale economics are usually highly important for Supply Network Architects in achieving superior efficiency. This position often competes with Product Innovators and Relationship Owners for customers' business, and neither of those two competing positions is primarily focused on low cost—providing an opportunity for the Supply Network Architect to win at the cost game. In fact, in the earlier days of strategic frameworks, "low cost" itself was often identified as a pure-form strategy. The problem is, without the complementary value drivers of network positioning and process leadership, low cost alone tends to be unsustainable over the long term; it is better thought of as just an *element* of the Supply Network Architect model.

The fabric of Supply Network Architect businesses is all about process efficiency, excellence of operations, and consistency of performance. Process metrics are established and the business is managed to the metrics. Enterprise training programs receive particular emphasis, as do simple but effective enterprise-wide modes of communications. Project management skills are cultivated and rewarded, as is the ability to effectively scale up processes. The culture is pragmatic and action oriented. When they do an acquisition, it is very clear who the acquirer is. They get on with things. In the energy space, for example, Exxon is the master of the Supply Network Architect position by virtue of its scale advantages and standardized, efficient global processes.

The three core value drivers of the Relationship Owner position are (surprise!) customer relationships, demand chain management, and optimizing scope. Clearly, the customer relationship itself is the most important of all—if this relationship is disrupted, the value capture potential of this position is seriously degraded. IBM, in its heyday of the 1970s, was an example of the master of this position. However, when this position was eroded by the technology disruptions of the 1980s, IBM's value capture declined significantly (IBM has since partially recaptured the position).

The demand chain management value driver refers to the effective management of the chain (or more generally, network) of activities that delivers product to the customer. The Relationship Owner does not actually need to own any of this chain; in fact, it is generally advisable not to, as the process of producing products and services requires very different competencies than owning customer relationships. Nevertheless, the Relationship Owner is *accountable* to the customer for delivery and therefore must be very effective in *managing* the demand chain.

The Relationship Owner position is driven by the economics of *scope*, as opposed to the economics of *scale* for the Supply Network Architect. A company in the Relationship Owner position never wants to be out-scoped by a competitor, as that may enable the competitor to establish a broader, and stronger, relationship with the customer. On the other hand, the scope can be extended too far, although this is less likely to be fatal as opposed to having insufficient scope. We can see this dynamic in action with Amazon.com, which seeks to be the online retail relationship owner. In their quest to be successful in that position, they have broadened scope considerably over the years—their move to acquire the leader in online shoe sales, Zappos, is a recent example.[2]

The business fabric of the Relationship Owner is one of fanatical focus on the customer. It strives to know more about the customer than the customer knows about herself. It's about a high degree of customer intimacy—knowing the nuances and tastes of the customer, and the names and birthdays of the wife and kids. It may be a high-touch, person-to-person, people-intensive business, or like Amazon, it may simulate this high-touch approach through sophisticated, personalized systems. As in the case of the Product Innovators, creativity is important; only the creativity of Relationship Owners flows from their deep understanding of the customer. And like the Supply Network Architects, there is a strong focus on metrics; only the focus is primarily on metrics that reflect the business's direct impact on the customer, such as customer retention and satisfaction.

The key point to keep in mind is that there is no one best position on our tapestry. The value creation capability of any particular position is a function of what is happening in the entire business ecosystem. The ecosystem learns and adapts accordingly. If a particular position has produced outstanding performance in the past, there will be a lot of imitators. A crowded position reduces value for all of the businesses in that position, so what worked before may not work in the future—in fact, it is often just the opposite.

Lifecycles of the Fabric

Sometimes the greatest rewards may indeed lie at one of the three pure form business model positions. However, a business does not just magically arrive at this position, or any other desired position. It needs to journey to the position from elsewhere—usually from some intermediate position along our fabric. It is learning to successfully manage these inevitable migrations that separate the most successful companies from all of the others.

Businesses have a lifecycle, and as I mentioned, businesses typically start their lives as Product Innovators. They may stay in that position indefinitely—it is a very viable value creation position as long as the business stays advantaged with regard to its core value drivers. Apple is a good example— it started as a Product Innovator, and it still is a Product Innovator (particularly when Steve Jobs is on the job). Often, however, there are reasons to move to another position. Such movements should not be taken lightly because the core value drivers change, which means that the very business fabric itself—including people, processes, competencies, and culture—has to adjust.

When movements are relatively small, the changes in the value drivers will be relatively small. There will be a little less emphasis on some or all of the prior drivers of importance, and a little more emphasis on drivers associated with other positions that are now a bit closer. At any given point on our tapestry we have a kind of weighted average of value drivers—our extremes give a one hundred percent weighting to their three core value drivers and essentially zero to the core drivers of the other extremes. But for everywhere else but the extremes—the far more likely areas of our strategic tapestry that a company will find itself in—there will be some value drivers that have less than a one hundred percent emphasis, but greater than zero. You'll have to be good but not necessarily great at some things.

In the exact middle of the tapestry is the theoretical spot that is associated with a 50 percent level of emphasis on all nine of the core value drivers. So is this the stuck-in-the-middle, jack-of-all-trades, avoid-at-all-costs position? Maybe, especially if many others are also situated nearby. But remember, the value driver weightings are about the level of your *focus* on the value drivers of your choice. Our framework implicitly assumes that the extent of your ability for one hundred percent focus is realistically bounded at about three value drivers. Perhaps that seems modest, but historical reality suggests not.

But could this limit on your *capacity* for focus be overcome? Could you, for example, be better than your competition on the basis of *more* than three value drivers? Or could you become better than historical bounds permitted in the few value drivers for which you do choose to focus? Could you change a "this *or* that" choice to a "this *and* that" opportunity? It's possible—and you know by now there is only one way to do that—to learn to learn better! That's the strategic-level promise of the learning layer.

But even if we can break through traditional boundaries, our organizations will have to adapt, and we once again run into the reality and the virtue of fuzziness. To successfully adapt, our value drivers and our business fabric necessarily change by degree rather than in a completely either/or way. As much as Aristotle and some traditional schools of strategy might like to argue differently, that's the reality of business.

As an example, if we start to move from a pure Product Innovator position toward a Supply Network Architect position, some compromises and tuning will be required. There will be a bit more emphasis on the *efficiency* of our product development. Perhaps we'll focus more attention on managing the supply chain that provides inputs to our products. These movements, even when slight, will be uncomfortable. It will feel to people like some *principles* of the business are changing. "Weren't we all about the product and its quality, and now suddenly we're starting to talk about how much it costs to make? It was always unconditional that the product came first before." Yes, but the world changed, and now there is competition for these products. Maybe you can innovate your way completely back to where you were, or maybe you simply are going to have to accept that you will always have to be a bit more cost conscious than before.

Small movements are generally relatively easy, but they may not get the competitive job done. Big movements are much more challenging because the fabric of the business has a significant inertia to it. It is therefore not surprising that the vast majority of businesses that make the attempt are not successful in moving to a new position far removed from their previous one. The businesses that are successful are some of the outstanding value creation stories in business. Let's take a quick look at some successful and not so successful migrations (figure 10.3).

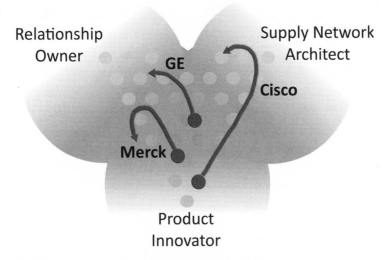

Figure 10.3 Lifecycles of the Business Fabric

Consider the famous case of Wal-Mart. Sam Walton had a better idea for retailing in 1962 when he opened his first store. He was a Product Innovator. Gradually, over the years, as Wal-Mart expanded, it differentiated itself more and more on the basis of process. Wal-Mart optimized efficiency through both highly innovative techniques and uncompromising standardization. It developed clear process leadership in multiple key areas of its business. And eventually, it was able to shape the entire supply network it participated in—wresting value from the formerly dominant manufacturers in the network and delivering more value to its customers than they could attain through other channels. As the world's largest retailer, Wal-Mart is now in a position such that the entire ecosystem around them dances to their tune.

As a very recent example of this power, Wal-Mart has begun imposing its will in its supply network by creating an environmental labeling program for all the products it sells that will require the products' producers to calculate and provide to Wal-Mart the environmental impact of their products.[3] Wal-Mart will then use this information to generate environmental ratings that will be displayed on the product, along with its price. This is not a program forced by the government on the supply chain (although it may be an attempt to address the issue before government inevitably does). Rather, this is a *mandate* from a Supply Network Architect gorilla that is creating a standard for its supply network that it believes will well serve Wal-Mart and its customers, and will just become another cost of entry for all those wanting to benefit from being in the Wal-Mart network.

Amazon started out as a Product Innovator as well. Jeff Bezos had a better idea about how to sell books by leveraging the newly available disruptive power of the Internet. It soon became very apparent, however, that the Internet was a potentially superior vehicle for establishing broad-ranging customer relationships across many different product categories. So Amazon rapidly migrated toward the Relationship Owner model by leveraging personalization capabilities, by offering a broader retail scope, and by assembling the infrastructure to effectively manage a massive demand network and customer fulfillment process.

Cisco Systems was likewise birthed on the basis of its founders' new product idea—the network router. However, it rapidly distinguished itself from similar technology companies by developing superior and highly scalable processes. Cisco is a company that has been very influenced by some of the top venture capitalists in the world—VCs who saw to it early in its history that Cisco would assemble arguably the top management team in Silicon Valley. In particular, Cisco brought in executives with superior process expertise, including the ability to debottleneck and scale processes, particularly in the areas of marketing, customer service, and mergers and acquisitions (M&A). Cisco was therefore able to manage through the hyper-growth of the 1990s more effectively than its competitors. By the late 1990s, Cisco was a master architect of its business ecosystem—the quintessential Supply Network Architect.

General Electric (GE) is an example of what was at the time (the 1980s) a loose collection of relatively undifferentiated businesses that Jack Welch turned into a performance powerhouse, fueled in large degree by the financial solutions "glue" of GE Capital. This was a company that truly was stuck in the middle, but got the leader they needed to steer the ship in the direction needed. GE certainly did not become a pure play Relationship Owner by any means, but by sailing north on our tapestry and then nudging a little more toward the Relationship Owner position, GE was able to reward its shareholders very handsomely.

On the other hand, the leading pharmaceuticals company Merck is an example of a premier product company that felt forced in the 1990s to begin moving, through acquisition, toward a Relationship Owner model in the face of buyer-side consolidation (i.e., health insurance consortia). When this movement did not yield favorable results, Merck attempted to back track toward their original position. Unfortunately, they failed to keep up with their competition in the product development arena that had historically been their strength and subsequently experienced a competitive decline.

These are just a few examples. The world in which businesses operate evolves over time, and so businesses must adapt accordingly. You can no doubt plot the journey of your own business over time on our tapestry, or think about how your business fabric would have to change if you moved in different directions. This is not a book primarily focused on business strategy, so we won't linger at length on the details of when and how to change strategic positions. What we will examine in some depth is the warp and weft of the fabric of various positions of our tapestry. We will particularly delve into the processes and practices that are of most importance to the fabric of businesses situated in different sections of our tapestry, and examine how the learning layer can be integrated into and strengthen the very fibers of this fabric.

11

Learning and Value

We have previously touched on some of the types of applications for which the learning layer can deliver new levels of value regardless of where your organization is, or is moving toward, on our tapestry. The "bread and butter" application is simply applying the learning layer to take the knowledge-based parts of your organization to the next level of performance. And this happens to dovetail quite well with the current agendas of senior business executives. As mentioned earlier, executives definitely get the point that the competitiveness of their business is all about accelerating intellectual capital development—it's the *how* you actually do it that has been a source of frustration.

IT leaders, laggards that we are sometimes accused of being, are also clearly on board with this agenda: according to *CIO* magazine's recent survey of senior IT executives, the top three areas of IT that they are actively researching are content and document management, collaboration and knowledge management, and business process management.[1] These are clearly all oriented toward improving the productivity of the knowledge-based workforce. Of course, although couched in the terminology of traditional and artificially separated technology categories, from our illuminated vantage point we can see that the solution they are actually groping for is our learning layer!

So there is certainly always an underlying need for better learning in any knowledge-based organization, whatever the specific fabric of the business. But we can gain some deeper insights on learning layer applications by explicitly recognizing that some activities in a business, and the projects within which they reside, are *predominantly* about learning. In fact, most generally, every project, and even every activity within a project, can be thought of as having *two* different sources of value. The first source of value is the *direct* value of the project itself. This will typically be measured as a present value of the future cash flows that the project is expected to generate. This is the quantified value of a project that everyone is familiar with.

But there is also always a *second* source of value: the additional information, and more importantly, the derived *learning* from that information, the project will generate that will contribute toward more effective decisions with regard to future activities. So the *expected total value* of any activity or project is always the sum of its *expected direct value* and its *expected learning value*.

The value of the information generated, and the subsequent learning derived from it, is ultimately a function of the expected amount of *uncertainty* that the project will serve to reduce. And more specifically, the value comes from reducing an uncertainty such that a *different* decision would be made versus the case in which we did not have the benefit of the reduction in uncertainty. In other words, mathematically, information, and by extension, learning, only has value if it has the potential to *affect a decision*, large or small. This makes sense if you think about it—if an item of information will in no way affect a decision we are going to make, then that information really isn't worth anything to us. If, for example, we know for certain that no matter what an analysis we are considering conducting might show, we are *never* going to invest in a certain opportunity, then the value of the analysis is worth exactly zero. By the way, this way of thinking would seem to be a "no-brainer," yet it is amazing how often this simple logic is somehow ignored in corporations.

Now you might object to this rather mechanical sounding definition of learning: "But learning is about discovery, the art of the possible, creating and innovating, and a flash of insight; not simply reducing uncertainty!" Yes, learning is about discovering and creating, but ultimately, from a mathematical point of view, gaining such insights and breakthroughs have value because they amount to reducing uncertainty. It is sometimes hard for us to psychologically frame our creative work that way because we want to consider only one side of the learning coin: all of our emphasis is on *succeeding* in finding a solution. In other words, we strive to create certainty that we can, in fact, do something—and we can do that by actually *finding* a solution. We are often not very interested in demonstrating something is actually *impossible*; so there is an aspirational asymmetry that clouds the reality that learning is at its core about reducing uncertainty, or equivalently, enhancing predictability. In fact, if something is actually impossible, it is valuable to know that as soon as possible. If you're destined to fail, it's cheaper to fail early!

But it turns out that this more mathematical, decision analytic-based trail of logic just leads us to exactly the same conclusion as David Garvin and other learning theorists who have come at the issue from a more classical organizational behavior perspective—organizational learning that really matters must ultimately inform behaviors and lead to something *actionable;* that is, we do something different on the basis of the learning than we would otherwise do.

By the way, in this book I typically reserve the term "value of information" (also sometimes referred to as the "value of clairvoyance") to be associated with a particular *uncertainty*. Generally that implicitly means the value of *perfect* information—that is, the value of knowing with one hundred percent certainty a future outcome. This is in a sense an idealized, upper bound on the value of predictability associated with the uncertain variable. But for the value of specific *actions* that can be taken to reduce the uncertainty, I will use the term "expected learning value" of the action. The result of such an action will still typically leave us short of perfect foresight, so the expected learning value of an action is usually a value of *imperfect* information associated with an uncertainty. Mathematically it is all the same, but I've found that the active term "learning" in the context of actual specific actions resonates better with most executives.

Now for some types of projects, the indirect, or expected learning value, will be pretty small. In other cases, it will be the lion's share of the expected value of the project. In fact, some projects will be *expected* to have a negative direct value, so that it is up to the learning value to outweigh this cost. We have some everyday labels for those types of projects and activities—R&D, or even more specifically, experiments.

The Value Zones of Learning

Generalizing these concepts, we can construct an "expected total value" diagram (figure 11.1) that graphically summarizes, on the basis of the relative magnitude of the two sources of value, the different types of projects that are found across the portfolio of any business.

In accordance with the dual sources of project value, the two axes of the diagram are (1) the expected direct value of

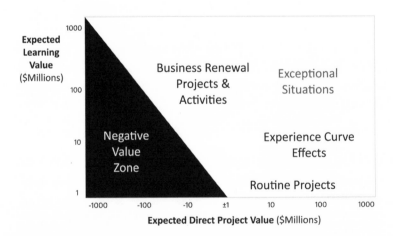

Figure 11.1   The Zones of Learning Value

a project, and (2) the corresponding expected learning value of the project. Both axes are in terms of the present value of future cash flows, and for convenience of applicability to businesses and projects of a broad range of sizes, the scales of both axes are log-based. The direct project value can potentially be negative in value, while learning value cannot be negative—information can be worthless if it does not ultimately affect a decision as we saw above, but it cannot be negative in value (we'll ignore pathological cases!).

Now let's examine the major sections of the expected total value diagram in a little more detail. First, you'll notice the dark triangle on the left—that's the negative value zone. That is the area in which the direct value of the project is negative, and the learning value is insufficient to make up for this negative value. This is the province of disastrous R&D money pits big and small, usually a result of unwarranted escalation of commitment or just neglect, and projects in this area should be shut down immediately. Just say no!

Opposite that triangle of gloom is the zone in the lower right that comprises the bulk of a business's projects; those in which the direct value significantly outweighs the learning value. For very routine projects and activities, the learning value may be negligible. More often, particularly for knowledge-intense organizations, there is some learning gained while conducting these projects that will be applicable to more efficiently or effectively execute future projects of a fairly similar nature. This type of learning comes under the general heading of "experience curve effects." Learning value of this kind tends to taper off as more projects of the same type are conducted, but never quite goes to zero.

There is an area above the more routine projects on our diagram in which only exceptional projects fall. These are projects in which the expected direct value is positive and the expected learning value is significant as well—to the extent of making up a large proportion of the total value of the project. At first blush you might assume this happy state of affairs could happen reasonably often. But if you think about it in terms of learning only having value if it has the potential to affect a decision, you can see why these types of projects should be very rare. For if we already expect positive value for the project, then we would naturally assume positive value for other similar future projects, and so the outcome of this project would be unlikely to affect our future decisions (the default would be to "just do it!"), and hence the learning value must be low to nil.

An exception to this logic is that if the current project accrues special value because of *unique* circumstances that will not apply to similar future projects, then the expected learning value may indeed be high. An example of this would be a situation in which a current R&D-type project qualifies for a credit that substantially helps its economics, but the credit is not expected to be applicable to future projects of a similar type. So, again, exceptional cases only in this region.

The last region is of particular interest from a learning standpoint—*business renewal* projects and activities. This is the wedge roughly in the left-center of the diagram in which the expected learning value outweighs the expected direct value of the project. Most often the expected direct value will be negative, but that is not necessarily always the case; it is just that the learning value is by far the *predominant* source of value. For example, small-scale entrepreneurial endeavors can sometimes be expected to have a least a modest positive direct value (hope springs eternal!), but the first steps are really about learning enough to successfully scale to a much bigger play. More typically, and realistically, however, business renewal activities will have a negative direct value—they are really just a business's costs of sustenance and growth.

Business renewal projects and activities that serve to grow and revitalize the business, include, for example, technology R&D, demonstrations, market analysis, and business and competitive intelligence, to name just a few. These are the projects and activities to which special attention must be paid if we are to accelerate our business's intellectual capital as they contribute a disproportionate amount to the business's stock of knowledge. Because R&D traditionally connotes product development activities, we may be tempted to think that business renewal is primarily of concern to Product Innovators. But obviously business renewal activities will be found in every business regardless of their particular position on our tapestry—it's just that the nature of the business renewal activities will be different. So given its tremendous leverage on learning value, we will dive deep on business renewal-related processes and organizations in conducting our overview of learning layer applications.

12

Business Renewal and Innovation

You have probably by now already considered some ways the learning layer can contribute to your organization's *general* ability to learn more efficiently and effectively. We'll now go further and explore *specific* learning layer application opportunities as we travel together across our strategic tapestry. We'll examine applications of the learning layer in the context of value drivers, processes, and practices that are particularly relevant for organizations whose fabric corresponds to particular portions of our tapestry. And we'll pay particular attention to applications to amplify the learning associated with experience curve effects, as well as with business renewal-related projects and processes.

In these travels we will see that in some cases the learning layer serves to enhance existing processes and practices. In other areas, we will find that there are opportunities for a whole new set of best practices that can be enabled by imaginatively applying the learning layer. And it should be remembered that most of the applications we will review can apply to *any* organization—it is just that they may be particularly transformational or are likely to lead to the greatest competitive advantages when associated with particular value drivers, and by extension, particular business model positions.

For organizations whose fabric most resembles our Product Innovator, it is critical that they consistently have demonstrably better products (or services) than their competition, and since the lifecycle of a truly superior product is generally fairly short, and the economic rewards are highest at the *beginning* of the lifecycle, the time-to-market is also critical. Consequently, the performance of business renewal processes such as R&D and, most generally *innovation*, are of paramount concern. We'll therefore spend a good deal of time exploring the ways in which the learning layer, combined with some new process approaches, can be truly transformational for renewing the business. And while we launch this discussion with an eye toward the Product Innovator, as I have already stressed, this transformation of business renewal applies equally as well to businesses residing just about anywhere else on our tapestry (figure 12.1).

It is often underappreciated that innovation is most fundamentally an information management process. Very little

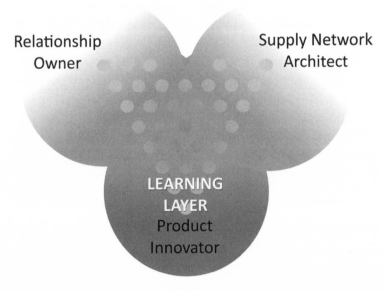

Figure 12.1 Applying the Learning Layer to Innovation and Renewal

is created *de novo*—innovations invariably build off previous ideas and innovations.[1] It is mathematically all about combinatorics. As Kary Mullis, who won the Nobel prize for his invention of the revolutionary polymerase chain reaction (PCR), the ingenious amplification technique that underlies modern genetic applications, put it: "In a sense, I put together elements that were already there, but that is what inventors always do. You can't make up new elements usually. The new element, if any, was the combination, the way they were used . . ."[2]

But unfortunately in most of today's larger organizations there are some very basic issues that get in the way of fully harnessing the power of creative combinatorics. For example, it is typically the case that the would-be innovator has very limited visibility of know-how and other capabilities inside or outside her organization on which to build valuable innovations. And let's face it; a particular issue in many R&D organizations is that there is often a relatively meager interest in actually sharing results. These organizations are populated by very smart, highly opinionated, and high-cost-of-time individuals—a workforce profile that I have found is highly correlated with social environments in which the general sharing of knowledge can be quite low!

The learning layer can help overcome this opaqueness of the pool of existing knowledge by providing a *transparent* environment in which knowledge assets can be organized and recombined in ways that sustainably support the creative process. And with its array of learning metrics, the learning layer strongly incentivizes sharing among even the most hard-bitten researchers by providing a built-in way to achieve on a *continuous* basis recognition and positive feedback that can rival the more traditional and episodic gratification received through external publications or patents.

These are some of the very basic ways the learning layer can boost the creative engine of your enterprise. But there is more, much more. The *overall process* for generating, developing, evaluating and making funding decisions can be transformed by a learning layer environment![3] "What," you say, "a *process*—for innovation?" Yes, this is where the adaptive nature of the learning layer comes through for us by enabling the process plasticity, flexibility, and personalization that has been so missing from the processes of the past, overcoming the sense of brittleness that made "process" such a dirty word in the hallways of the Product Innovator. But the opportunity is broader than "just" innovation—it's about being as effective as possible at *renewing* the business, about growth and sustainability. And that's certainly relevant to all businesses, whether or not you make widgets, and regardless of your position on our tapestry.

Business Renewal in Perspective

Before leaping to a solution, however, let's take some time to set the context of the "as-is" business development processes in most companies. Since about the mid-1990s, corporate development processes have been considerably influenced by the approaches of commercial VCs. This influence, of course, reached a crescendo at the height of the Internet bubble. Silicon Valley in particular, with its dynamic mix of venture capital and entrepreneurs, was lionized as a model from which traditional companies could learn to supercharge innovation and business development. Although we have since entered a more sober era, thousands of companies have been inspired to apply the techniques of venture capital to their business development and innovation processes, and to empower their rank and file employees to be the entrepreneurs—to be the grass roots source of more and better business ideas. And why not? It seems almost a "no-brainer" that it has to be a better way than traditional, bureaucratic-laden approaches.

Unfortunately, these corporate Silicon Valleys have generally delivered underwhelming results. How can that possibly be? Replacing legacy development and budgeting processes with the staged decisions and investment approaches of VCs certainly seems appealing. And more development ideas should clearly be a good thing. It is certainly not for lack of enough trying of the new model; I have found that, in fact, most companies I have become familiar with have embraced this general approach.

They have dutifully built their business idea "funnels" (and many explicitly describe in words and in images these processes as a funnel) on the basis of venture capital analogies. Although they vary in detail, these implementations almost all have the core characteristic of employing the metaphor of a funnel in which raw business ideas enter one end of the funnel, and at various stages along the funnel decisions are made as to whether to fund the next stage of the idea. The process is obviously described as a funnel because it conveys the notion that ideas get continuously weeded out over time, just as VCs fund only a very small percentage of business plans that they review, and continue to fund an even smaller proportion.

What I have also found, however, is that in the corporate environment very little tends to come out of the other end of the funnel. In fact, I have often seen literal depictions of funnels on the walls of corporate business development centers, with the flow of opportunities typically oriented left-to-right. The problem is usually not that there are insufficient ideas being generated. Indeed, the left (flared) side of the funnel is often chock-full of ideas. But very little is shown emerging from the far right of the funnel, indicative of successful products, services, or ventures launched. What is worse is that although not much comes out of these funnels, they still seem to somehow consume large sums of capital!

Clearly then, many companies are deriving much less value than originally expected from these exercises. Furthermore, employees often see the process as demotivating because of the paucity of positive results. They eagerly bought into the grass roots idea generation process that has been so strongly advocated by just about every management book on the topic of the past 20 years. Yet, they do not see much in the way of results from all of their creativity.

The programs can, in fact, seem like a cruel hoax to these employees, sabotaging the original intention of promoting enhanced employee empowerment and motivation, as well as the harnessing of broad-based creativity.

Why have these processes gone so astray? The roots of the problem lie in a misunderstanding of the nature of value creation within a standard business versus value creation facilitated by commercial VCs. And it is compounded by a lack of appreciation that innovation, and therefore business renewal, for larger organizations is fundamentally a problem of effective information and knowledge management.

Let's review the basics of venture capital. The primary role of the VC is the assessment of external business ideas and their potential to translate into superior returns. The VC then provides capital to those few business ideas and associated management teams that they judge as having the ability to return adequate value to their investors within the desired time horizon. The expected return needs to be quite high to compensate for the very high risk associated with investing in unproven business concepts. Although VCs sometimes provide some ongoing guidance to their funded companies, that is not their primary role. Nor do they traditionally have any role whatsoever in the actual development of business ideas, or of finding useful synergies and linkages among business ideas.

Let's contrast this with corporate business renewal processes—the processes focused on sustenance and growth whose primary source of value is their expected learning value. So how should corporate business renewal processes differ from the processes of VCs? First, unlike VCs, the fabric of most corporations includes lots of existing capabilities of many types, both tangible and intangible. In the parlance that we will define in more detail below, corporations own and have access to a primordial soup of "capability components"—units of tangible and intangible assets that constitute realized or potential technologies, physical assets, processes, people, IP, and relationships. This is very different from a venture capital firm, and this difference alone suggests that the traditional VC approach is not the best model for corporate business renewal processes.

Second, corporate business renewal processes must serve to explicitly discover and exploit synergies *among* various business ideas and capability components. In other words, the job is not to just *assess* ideas as in the case of VCs—the job is to also *generate* business ideas. And in particular, to generate valuable ideas that leverage the company's *unique collection* of capability components.

Third, corporate business renewal processes must continuously work to adjust and *improve* business ideas over time—not to just fund them. It's relatively easy to brainstorm up raw business ideas and provide some seed funding. It's a whole lot harder to feed and care for them to successful commercialization, and in a manner such that the success is demonstrable to the parent organization. Again, this adds to the much greater scope of responsibilities of corporate business renewal processes compared with the activities of VCs.

Companies that bought into the simple venture capital analogy typically assign some executive teams to act as funding decision makers, and within the business renewal process that's essentially their only responsibility. Unfortunately, the business idea generation part of the process is often relegated to a glorified suggestion box. The explicit examination of synergies among business ideas and capability components is typically ad hoc at best. And, finally, adjustments to business ideas once they have entered the funnel tend to be minimal.

The result is that lots of grass root ideas may enter the funnel, but with each idea assessed in a stand-alone and essentially static manner, at some point any given business idea is likely to get killed. It should be no surprise, then, that nothing much comes out of the end of the funnel, and companies have come to feel let down by their processes for renewing their business. This in turn inevitably leads to hostility from the "core" units of the business toward the areas that are responsible for delivering "new" ideas, and that spend the core's hard earned profits doing so. Ultimately, when times get sufficiently tight, the core refuses to fund the "pipe dreams" any longer and the funnel collapses.

A Fabric of a Different Nature

So what's the solution to funnels that don't deliver? Keep the funnel, but flip it around! That is, business renewal needs to be a process of *learning* that continuously increases valuable options and opportunities—the funnel needs to flare out over time, not taper off. It needs to be transformed into a *generative* process, not primarily just an *eliminative* process (figure 13.1). It needs to build on and integrate with the capabilities of the core business.

But to do this requires the application of a real, learning layer-enabled *process*, not just "throwing ideas on the wall, and seeing what sticks." The VC-inspired, but mostly ad hoc approaches that typify current business renewal processes in most companies are simply not good enough to deliver the business renewal goods. At the scale of the enterprise, advantages versus competitors in the business renewal arena are gained on the basis of superior processes, information management and organizational learning, not just more creative people. You need your business renewal processes to continuously generate *informational advantages* versus not only competitors, but versus all the other participants in your business's ecosystem.

But wait, you say, won't all this systematizing stifle out-of-the-box thinking and creativity? It's actually just the opposite! Innovation may be a function of creative combinatorics, but the vast majority of combinations are no more than hopeful monsters. It is the ability to massively broaden the

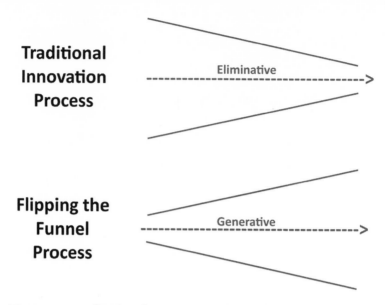

Figure 13.1   Flipping the Business Renewal Funnel

scope of the combinations in an intelligent, value-driven way and to then dive deep into the combinatorial patterns that exhibit the most promise that leads to innovations that matter. And that only comes from a strong cumulative base of *learning*.

I once saw a program in which an awestruck interviewer asked the virtuoso violinist Itzhtak Perlman how he was able to be so very creative with the violin. Perlman shook his head and chuckled, and then recounted all of the many years of his of life in painstaking and rigorous training and practice—emphasizing the point that to be truly creative, you must first know discipline in your craft. And as Kary Mullis articulated from his personal inventive experience, the reality of innovation is that it is not only an exercise in connections and combinations, but that very little of even the most significant of innovations is likely to be entirely new. Rather, it is generally a matter of recombining existing elements in new ways. Which is why some of the greatest inventions can seem fairly obvious in hindsight, and elicit a "Why didn't I think of that?" reaction.

By the way, I definitely don't want to give the impression that these knowledge-based, more systematic approaches to innovation and learning should replace the popular programs that focus on individual and team creativity that have been in vogue for some time—these programs are clearly complementary, and can indeed be necessary to achieve the best possible results. But to expect that type of generalized training to be *sufficient* to generate valuable outcomes from large-scale business renewal processes is sort of like expecting those kinds of programs alone to enable a novice musician to compose a great symphony, and then play it with a single violin.

So, is all of what I'm advocating here entirely new? Naturally, of course, some companies have employed elements of what I'm advising, but under different names. A good example of the transformational implications of the combinatorial direction in innovation is the rational drug design processes of pharmaceutical companies. Historically, pharmaceutical development was essentially a trial and error art form, but now drugs are more systematically designed. The key to this approach is to be able to efficiently search through as many combinations as possible, and then to identify those with the highest value potential. It is an approach that requires a whole new level of information management, along with much greater process discipline.

Another example is GE. Although it was not explicitly termed as such, elements of what was essentially a flipping-the-funnel process seemed to have played a role in the success of GE. For example, here are some relevant retrospective comments by Jack Welch: "Linkage is expansion.... With linkage, you're seeing how an idea has mushroomed between meeting A, when you first brought it up, and meeting B, when you ask about it again.... That's what linkage is—ideas getting enriched from one meeting to the next."[1] This sounds an awful lot like the essence of a flipped funnel approach. And what is significant about GE is that their "flipped funnel" included ideas and capabilities from *anywhere*—Welch's famous "boundaryless" approach—enabling the GE flipped funnel to immensely increase its potential value. This is a solid, sensible approach of the kind that you would expect from GE—maybe not including all the details discussed here, but on the same track. But, of course, what this historical GE process did not have the benefit of is being infused with our learning layer, with innovation and learning visibly flowing, and processes adapting to circumstance. That's the new opportunity!

A Fabric Unbraided

So what exactly is the process of flipping a funnel? It starts with *decomposing* raw business ideas into units that can be effectively worked on in a systematic way. Business ideas or opportunities themselves are often too coarse grained to enable the deep, generative processes required. We need to decompose them into capability components, which you will recall are units of tangible and intangible assets that constitute realized or potential production assets, technologies, processes, people, IP, and relationships. The more fine grained the capability components, the more interesting and valuable the combinations that can be developed. And these capability components and related descriptions can be represented as topical areas and knowledge assets within our learning layer. Basically, what we are doing is unbraiding a relevant patch of the capabilities aspect of our business fabric in preparation for a process of beneficial reweaving.

Importantly, the value of capability components is often a function of their ability to serve as part of a solution that can add immediate business value, and at the same time as a function of their ability to enable potentially multiple future innovations. In other words, there is an *option value* element to every capability component, and the flipped funnel methodology can explicitly recognize this often-overlooked element of value.

Some types of capability components are obvious, but others are quite often overlooked. For example, in science and engineering-driven companies, "softer" components such as relationships are often given short shrift. Also, the capability components to be considered should include not only those currently "owned" by the business, but also those that could be developed by the company in the future, and importantly, those that are currently owned by third parties.

What we are accomplishing with this decomposition technique is simply what innovators like Kary Mullis do intuitively and individually. They break things down into their essential features, and then try to visualize the effect of different combinations, orientations, and application approaches. We want to be able to do the same thing, except on the enterprise level, where everyone can effectively participate in the creative agenda, where we can actually harness social scale advantages in the process of innovation—a process that has been traditionally thought of as one of *diseconomies* of scale, surrendered by default to that rare individual inventive genius or the odd small group.

Most business ideas are a *bundle* of two or more of our capability components. For example, even if a business idea is based on a technological breakthrough, the overall opportunity is likely to also include other differentiating components, such as processes (say, a specific marketing process). It is the uniqueness of the *bundle of components* that provides the economic value-creating potential of the idea, and the ability to defy the easy copying by other marketplace participants that leads to rapid value collapse.

Once a first-cut decomposition of potential ideas or solutions is conducted (figure 13.2), the capability components

Figure 13.2   Decomposing the Traditional Funnel

can be organized so that key *leverage* points can be identified. This is fundamentally an exercise in gaining insights into the ways individual or collections of capability components can enable multiple business ideas. At the same time we can also understand which sets of business ideas have *synergy* through common capability components.

In some applications, subsets of capability components may influence economically important variables of a potential opportunity. For example, we assisted an engineering-based client in developing a network of influencing capabilities, some existing and some to be developed, that collectively could improve a critical operating variable by 200 percent. But many of these same capability components also benefited other, quite different opportunities. As in this case, there are often multiple, overlapping networks of influencing capabilities, with the value of each capability component being a function of all of the opportunities and options that they could potentially influence. Whether the key variables being influenced relate to the efficacy of a drug, the heat dissipation of an electronic device, or the yield of a biofuel process, the method is the same.

A medium to large company will have at least hundreds of business ideas, each with at least dozens of capabilities, so clearly this process becomes an exercise in effective information and knowledge management. Is this tough to do well? Yes. Do VCs have to do this? No. But, if you run a business of any size, there is simply no other way to squeeze every last bit of value out of your assets and intellectual capital. And besides, if it was too easy there would no way to gain an advantage!

And this is where the learning layer comes in. As we decompose opportunities into capability components, what should we automatically be thinking about? We should be thinking that these capability components, and associated documents and other descriptive information, can and should be represented as topics and knowledge assets. And that there are *relationships* among these capability components as well as between the capability components and the original ideas and opportunities from which they are decomposed. And that the relationships are not necessarily of the same type, and may be by degree. In other words, what we really have within our funnel is a *fuzzy network* of opportunities and capability components. Some of the capability components that are represented as knowledge assets will be people. So our entire funnel can actually be represented by our architecture of learning, the integrated fuzzy knowledge and social network.

A Fabric Rewoven

Although we are by no means finished with the overall flipping-the-funnel process, invariably significant dividends begin to accrue even at this stage of the process. First of all, we nearly always find that the process uncovers key leverage points that have been missed because previously the company's business development activities were operating primarily within specific organizational silos. The flipping-the-funnel process promotes greater integration across organizational boundaries, and reveals the synergies that would otherwise be missed.

Perhaps even more importantly, information advantages begin to be achieved versus other players in the company's business "ecosystem." For example, high leverage third party relationships may be identified—high leverage by virtue of the relationships potentially enabling *multiple* business ideas. This knowledge can provide insights on the potential value of the third party that the third party may not even be aware of itself! Which means a favorable deal can be potentially struck with the third party before others catch on. In general, the flipping-the-funnel process can reveal the latent value of assets, relationships, and people that may not yet be recognized by the overall market, or by any other individual market participant. This favorable information asymmetry can enable you to lock-in advantages that would otherwise be missed or lost to other players.

The other major advantage of flipping the funnel is that detailed information on capability component *leverage* enables a more intelligent process of investment. Investments can be staged and funded so as to ensure the greatest opportunity for value. Through a process of continuously looking ahead, and then working backwards, the staging can be optimized. As capability components are developed, business ideas take shape. These are continuously prototyped and evaluated. If they continue to look attractive, they move forward toward commerciality. If not, they are adjusted, recombined with other ideas, or halted. The result is a flipped funnel that generates a much greater number of successful products, solutions, or ventures, as well as providing options for many more, compared to the classic funnel.

Your legacy, classic development funnel(s) need not be thrown out. Rather a new parallel flipped funnel can be developed. In fact, these funnel approaches can coexist; the traditional funnel can be a source of new business ideas that can be systematized, adjusted and staged appropriately within the flipped funnel.

But the legacy funnels will not be your only source of raw business ideas—the flipped funnel itself is a superior process for harnessing organizational creativity that yields real results. Again—innovation is about combinations. And the flipped funnel process provides an infrastructure for identifying and filtering vastly more combinations than just leaving it to ad hoc processes. It is beyond the scope of this book, but innovation "operators" can be applied in a systematic way to sets of capability components to maximize the innovation potential.[2] But what *is* within our remit here is to make the point that when the learning layer is helping to manage the flipping-the-funnel business renewal process, its adaptive recommendations of relevant people and knowledge assets will ensure that even more relevant combinations and patterns will be considered.

The new ideas generated within the flipped funnel process have a more realistic chance of being funded and leading to ultimate commercial success because they are much more likely to leverage high option value capability components

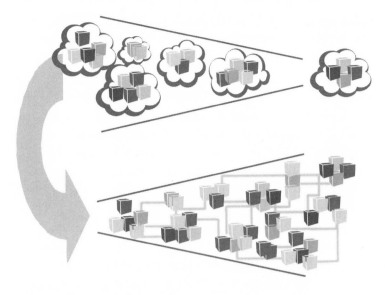

Figure 13.3   Flipping the Funnel in Action

than are ideas generated by ad hoc means. This implies your investment program will be much more efficient in its use of capital. These new business ideas generated within the flipped funnel are in turn decomposed into the capability components and then integrated into the overall investment staging program (figure 13.3).

As investment opportunities are added to the flipped funnel, the process of staging, evaluating, recombining and creating continues. Options continuously increase, which leads to tangible value. In addition, commercially successful ventures are much more likely to emerge. Implementation is more realistic, and requires shorter lead times, than in the case of the traditional funnel approach because sufficient capability development will have already been done through intelligent look ahead.

Flipping the Funnel in Practice

I've had the opportunity to flip around some funnels in a number of organizations. One example is a large, technically proficient company that has long been a pioneer in enhanced business development processes. The company had adopted a venture capital-style funding approach, and had established forums for enhancing the generation of new business ideas. This was a clear advance over its traditional approaches, and delivered some immediate successes. It was rapidly adopted throughout the company's vast network of businesses, serving as a cornerstone of its business development processes.

Notwithstanding this early success, the company found that its business development processes were not consistently delivering the quantity of valuable new ventures that senior executives desired to meet aggressive new growth targets. Too few of the myriad ideas that entered the various business development funnels were making it to implementation. They decided it was time to once again raise the bar on their business development process.

Our firm, ManyWorlds, began working with one of the company's business units on an enhanced business renewal process—one that essentially flipped the funnels. We went well beyond the simple venture funding process by putting in place an integrative process *environment* to accelerate strategic innovation and venture implementation. The overall philosophy driving this approach was that innovation is really about combinations—creating them, evaluating them, positioning them, and continuously adjusting them. The process environment was designed to significantly enhance the identification of unfulfilled marketplace needs, and to facilitate matching and evaluating those needs against different combinations drawn from a comprehensive set of capability components.

ManyWorlds assisted the company in building a prototype learning network that included the appropriate supporting technology platform, knowledge architectures, process flows and process toolkits to facilitate the flipped funnel approach. Soon, business renewal began to take on a more systematic and efficient look—and one that yielded results. Clusters of innovations were developed that leveraged common components, resulting in much greater efficiency along with a more realistic shot at successful execution.

Another example where we flipped a funnel was an R&D organization that had a number of unique competencies in the general area of carbon management, but was stuck on how to develop a solution that would actually gain traction in the marketplace. The client had some initial ideas, some of which seemed to us like a solution looking for a problem, and others that were so wild and naïve that you couldn't help but smile. They were very smart people, but needed some help in weaving their competencies into distinct commercial value.

So our team looked at the nascent ideas they already had in place and helped them decompose these ideas into capability components. Then we canvassed their organization for other capability components that might come into play, including capabilities that did not currently exist but that they could develop, as well as potentially relevant capabilities that existed but that were not available within the four walls of their company. As is usual when we conduct these exercises, even though the core scientific domains of the capabilities in question were somewhat peripheral to the primary business of this company, the collection of capability components we amassed was much greater than anyone would have initially imagined. I have found this to be typical—the latent generative power hidden within just about every organization I have ever come across never ceases to surprise when it is finally fully revealed!

Having established our primordial soup of capability components, we took a step back and looked at a broad spectrum of relevant unfulfilled needs in the marketplace, many of which were only beginning to emerge. We did some fairly simple quantifications of the value that could accrue to relevant "idealized solutions"—solutions that might not currently be possible, and potentially might *never be fully* possible, but that would provide a sense of the potential upside. The team followed this up by developing some more realistic solutions that could potentially be implemented within a few years, and did some rough estimates on the value these partial solutions could generate. These were then mapped to our collection of capability components. As we did so, we began to create some additional solutions that hadn't been thought of before, and adjusted some of the original ones on the basis of the strengths and weaknesses of the capability components we had to work with. This allowed us to be more creative than we otherwise would have been because we had the discipline to first do the capability component work.

We moved from some early themes that they had regarding carbon trading and sulfur scrubbing technologies that were good ideas, but just didn't fit well with their capability component mix, much less their business fabric, to *solutions* based on environmental advisory matters and providing advice to carbon traders. These advisory-based solutions leveraged some common capability components, which provided synergy and cost effectiveness. And it turned out that some of their initial ideas, such as environmental remediation services, were keepers, which we were able to make crisper and more distinctive, as well as more efficient, through the leveraging of capability components that were common with the advisory-based solutions. In the course of generating these solutions, the team also identified a relatively obscure third party that had a particular competency that could be an important contributor to several of the solutions we had developed. This insight ultimately led to a valuable, privileged relationship with this party.

This was an example in which we focused most of our initial attention on capability components and got the components identified and organized, moved on to exploring marketplace needs, and then worked backward from these needs to our capability components, and creatively iterated from there. But in your application, the process could also start the other way, with market assessments and identification of unfulfilled needs, followed by working backwards toward idealized solutions, and only then beginning to address the capability component side of the equation. The beauty is you can start either way; you will necessarily converge to similar outcomes, and you will always generate a whole bunch of insights along the way that you wouldn't have otherwise had.

Tracking the Value

Although flipping the funnel is a creative process, there can, and usually should be, significant financial rigor built in to the process as well. We've applied the flipping-the-funnel process in environments in which there are myriad technical process pathways that have to be considered, but in which it is also clear that there will ultimately only be one pathway left standing—the low-cost pathway will eventually prevail in the marketplace. In such cases detailed financial models need to track along each step of the process, generating value projections on a continuous basis.

A case in point is an area in which we've had a good deal of client experience, cleantech—the term that describes climate change-friendly energy technologies. We've worked with emerging companies with a better widget or process to extract energy, as well as large utilities and energy companies who need to incorporate these technologies into their everyday operations. There are literally hundreds of different pathways spanning the renewable resources that the world provides us and the delivery of the energy to the consumer. It will take many years to sort it all out, but there is one reality that looms over the whole industry—the unit of renewable energy consumed will be a commodity, just like its fossil fuel predecessors. And as many of its pioneers have already discovered, economics will ultimately rule—a few pennies per gallon, and less than that per kilowatt hour, is going to separate the few ultimate winners from all the others that fall by the wayside.

So understanding the economics at every step of the value chain from the field to the consumer is critical, which means understanding the economic impact of all the relevant capability components in our creative broth is critical. For value chains in emerging areas such as renewable energy that are in a state of continuous construction, the learning layer is invaluable for ensuring ever-changing knowledge from within the organization and beyond, including the most current insights on relevant economics, is taken into consideration by those making specific, local, and rapid-fire decisions.

Optimizing Learning Value

To extend the learning benefits further in emerging fields and industries, we often incorporate an "experimental design" aspect to the flipped funnel approach. Experimental design is about effectively selecting and staging experiments, and again, as I mentioned, "experiments" is really just the label we all use for actions in which the source of value is solely the expected learning value. So experimental design boils down to trying to achieve the most learning for the least cost. Traditionally this kind of design is done in the bowels of the laboratory and is of fairly limited scope, if done at all. But the basic idea extends to any situation in which there are uncertainties, and there are actions (i.e., experiments) that can be undertaken to potentially reduce the uncertainties.

Many of our capability components will have significant uncertainties associated with them, and certainly the marketplace in which our solutions are targeted are filled with uncertainties. What is the expected lifecycle of the product, for example? How will the technology perform under various conditions? Do we think we will be able to do a deal to secure the rights to a key capability? What if the regulatory environment changes? Is it likely our competitors will preempt our plans? Sound financial modeling combined with a dose of decision analysis-based techniques can provide a quantifiable understanding of the value of information with regard to these types of uncertainties. This in turn enables a quantification of the *expected learning value* of *actions* that can be taken to at least partly reduce the uncertainties.

And it is important to remember that these actions may be of a more general information gathering nature than just classic scientific experimentation. They can include forecasting, IP analysis, market intelligence, and feeling out the interest level of a third party in partnering, for example. As the results from any of these types of actions are attained, the capability component map can be updated accordingly, and value models rerun. This process provides a closed loop between the flipped funnel and our information gathering and R&D experimentation activities.

I've seen this approach reverse what would otherwise be some very destructive decisions. For example, I have reviewed proof of concept and demonstration projects that were on the verge of being killed because routine pro forma financials had been generated, but not expected learning value quantifications. When properly looked at from the learning perspective it became clear the expected reductions in technology-related uncertainties that the demo would generate was worth much more than its admittedly substantial cost. I have also been involved in cases in which R&D budgets were hopelessly misaligned because there was little or no sense of the true value that various research programs would deliver. When we quantified the expected learning value we found that very large amounts of money were being spent on experimental programs that had relatively low informational leverage, whereas other areas that were being starved for funds would have a much greater economic impact.

In fact, what the approach quite typically uncovers is that there are uncertainties associated with factors that have profound economic consequences that are not being addressed by the traditional R&D programs, or by anyone else in the organization for that matter. These uncertainties are often of a general business nature and therefore fall into the white space of the organizations. Without a means for quantifying the magnitude of their impact against the costs of actions to abate the uncertainty, these issues tend to stay hidden in the white space until it's too late.

And while we are on the topic of financial value, perhaps a less obvious but nevertheless significant benefit of the flipped funnel approach is that it can tear down the traditional wall between investment in current operations and business renewal, overcoming the tyranny of the existing business that tends to eat its own children. Because the flipped funnel approach focuses on the constituent capability components and the *expected total value* of projects and activities, it is able to integrate across the world of the current and the world of the potential, and do so on an "apples to apples" basis. This is obviously important from a pure investment efficiency standpoint, but it also has cultural advantages. It maximizes the likelihood that new business ideas will not just be pie in the sky concepts that ultimately get shot down, but rather are ideas whose required capabilities can contribute immediate business benefits, in addition to providing solid options for the big future opportunity.

Unfolding Patterns of Value

The logical conclusion of the flipped funnel approach is that the locus of the management of the business becomes as much, or even more, about managing a mosaic of capabilities than just managing specific projects or opportunities. This is very beneficial because it reduces the risk of throwing the capability baby out with the opportunity bath water when the pursuit of an opportunity is stopped, and it maximizes the chance the capabilities and competencies that are *core* will be cultivated appropriately. In fact, it can help determine and provide organizational clarity on just what *is* core and *is not* core to a business. It is a deeper approach to managing the business than the traditional way—it is in a sense more about managing at the level of the true, underlying fabric of the business rather than just managing a particular set of episodic business opportunities.

What the flipped funnel process in combination with the learning layer also does at the business fabric level is to help ensure the building of the company's intellectual capital on a continuous basis. The identification, creation and evaluation processes within the flipped funnel processes are codified such that this enhanced base of knowledge has value in its own right. As Jack Welch suggested, your job as an executive, ". . . is about raising the fundamental intellect of the organization every day," and flipping the funnel combined with the learning layer provides a foundation for doing just that.[3]

And the learning layer contributes much more to the flipping-the-funnel process than just serving to help manage the capability component network. Its ability to derive learning from the collective wisdom of the community enables it to deliver adaptive recommendations of topics, knowledge assets and people that can accelerate innovation by sparking new ideas, and highlighting undiscovered connections. It encourages contributions of knowledge and insights that might not otherwise be made. It can serve as the platform for providing flexible process steps that is of assistance rather than being a barrier and a burden to the process participants. It can generate the metrics that can help provide an assessment of the efficacy of the innovation process. And it can help automatically maintain the overall innovation infrastructure through its intelligent self-modification features.

Embedding the flipping-the-funnel process within the learning layer is a powerful, contemporary approach to the management of innovation and R&D. But there are other related learning layer opportunities that should not be overlooked. For example, *technology transfer* processes. Here the idea is to enable third parties to leverage inventions and developments that are developed by other organizations, whether private or public. As mentioned previously, extending the learning layer across organizations is an ideal way to generate creative synergy. And the flipping-the-funnel approach can be adapted, and coupled with the cross-organizational learning layer, to enable more collaborative and valuable technology transfers.

I have argued that business renewal can be improved through systematic techniques, with the flipping-the-funnel process being a synthesis of such techniques. But innovation by its very nature will always be an emergent process, not fully predictable in its outcomes. Flipping the funnel amplifies this emergent quality of innovation—the output of the flipped enterprise funnel is much greater than the input. The output exceeds the sum of the inputs because the flipping-the-funnel process is the rare example of what the cognitive scientist and author Steven Pinker identifies as a *discrete combinatorial system*.[4] These are systems in which discrete elements are combined through the application of a set of recursive rules. Most phenomena in nature are not of this type—rather they are systems in which blending occurs and the discrete elements lose their identity. We know of, however, two discrete combinatorial systems in the natural universe: DNA and human language. Not coincidently, these systems have the unique capability of generating an endless stream of novelties through a combinatorics made infinite by the application of a kind of generative grammar—a grammar comprising a recursive set a rules for combining and extending the constituent elements.

Likewise, our learning layer is a discrete combinatorial system, recursively modifying itself and thereby yielding emergent properties, resulting in a form of a different nature than, and not fully predictable from, its individual inputs. When we weave the learning layer throughout and around our flipped funnel, we engineer an entirely new generative phenomenon from which emerges a brocade of valuable patterns of which we can only speculate beforehand, and marvel at as it unfolds before us. It's truly a fabric of a different nature.

Learning Layer Application Tour

We spent a good deal of time addressing business renewal, which for Product Innovators corresponds to their predominant value driver, product and service development; and we did a deep dive on what the marvels of the flipping-the-funnel process in combination with the learning layer can deliver against that value driver. But you will recall that there are a couple other important value drivers associated with Product Innovators: branding and distribution channels. These value drivers boil down to methods of getting the word out to potential customers on the benefits of their products and services, and then getting them into the hands of customers. It's basically an effective information transfer issue for the Product Innovator, and an issue of finding credible signals in a vast sea of noise for the potential customer.

You are probably familiar with some of the Web 2.0 techniques in this area—for example, leveraging customer advocates to promote viral marketing and to build and maintain a strong reputation. But learning systems can contribute even more. What are today just advertisements can become highly relevant adaptive recommendations, with detailed and credible explanations attached. The explanations can be made to authoritatively explain exactly why the business's products are the best fit for the specific recommendation recipient. And ordering the product is just a click-through away from the advertisement. The Product Innovator may not own the advertisement network itself, but it will have an incentive to ensure that its products and brand are promoted through advertisement networks and marketing channels that provide recipients this level of relevancy and credibility. Everyone wins with this approach—the Product Innovator gets a stronger message through to prospective customers, the advertising recipient gets more signal and less noise, and the advertising network provides a more valuable service.

Supply Network Architects

Let's now move up our business tapestry toward the Supply Network Architect position. I've worked with a lot of these types of companies, and I can attest to the fact that their people and processes are all about scale. They are often *very* large organizations (or want to be). So even though they are generally quite proficient in managing processes, their sheer size makes organizational learning a challenge. Some of the critical concerns of these types of organizations include large-scale project, process, and venture development and management, effective management of supplier networks, and merger and acquisition (M&A) support. We'll take a brief look at how the learning layer, with its unique capabilities for scalable learning, can play a role in taking these process areas to the next level of performance (figure 14.1).

Successful development and management of large-scale project, processes, and ventures really comes down to adapting and scaling up the flipping-the-funnel approach we have already reviewed. While there will generally be less emphasis on *product* innovation per se, there will be a strong focus on maximizing experience curve effects, and creatively, efficiently, and effectively combining the right *capabilities* at the right time for specific projects, processes and ventures. So we find again that the path to better business performance is all about effectively managing a capability network.

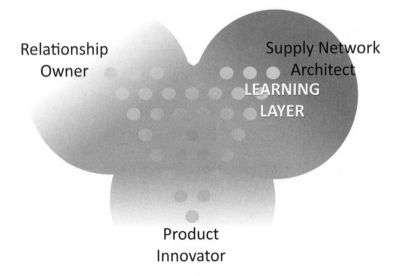

Figure 14.1 Building Learning into the Fabric of Supply Network Architects

Managing the required project capabilities has historically been done with databases, scheduling systems, and lots of planning sessions. And these will always be needed. The opportunity that the learning layer combined with our flipping-the-funnel process delivers is to facilitate a greater degree of *value-driven* innovation *within* the projects, and to promote a better flow of learning *across* projects and over time. Projects in technically demanding domains are rarely cookie cutter in nature. Efficiently replicating successes, as well as learning from failures, is the path to sustainably superior project management.

The problem with traditional methods of learning from previously conducted projects, or even from other projects in-progress, is that the noise inherent to the voluminous data generated from projects tends to overwhelm the learning signal of actionable insights. This has traditionally been addressed by nonsystem-based means, for example, through after-action reviews. This is an excellent approach, but has the shortcoming of being sufficiently time intensive that not all projects are likely to have a detailed formal review conducted, and not everyone in the organization is going to be able to directly participate in the reviews that *are* conducted. In either case, useful learning may not reach the people who are most in need of it and when it is most relevant to them.

The learning layer can supplement formal review processes by delivering real-time suggestions that point users to the insights required when they need them. These insights may consist, for example, of knowledge assets that are formal review documents that will be relevant to the user's particular situation. The learning layer's suggestions are likely to be of high relevancy because it can make inferences on the user's learning needs on the basis of its understanding of what similar users in similar situations have found relevant. In many cases the learning layer's suggestions will be of other *people* that appear to have had experiences that are likely to be relevant. This can put the user on the path toward additional knowledge assets that are relevant, or toward making direct contact with suggested people who can help. In any of these cases, the objective of the learning layer is to facilitate maximum learning while not wasting people's time. Supply Network Architects do not like to waste time!

They also do not like waste in their supply network. And they have an opportunity to extend the learning layer back through their supply network, thereby driving learning efficiency through the entire network they seek to effectively manage. For many years processes such as quality and inventory management have been extended by successful businesses throughout their supply network. Toyota is the well-known example of championing a supply network-wide quality process. Wal-Mart and other modern retailers have become masters at managing production and inventory throughout their supply networks. And there are other processes that leading Supply Network Architect businesses are beginning to extend throughout their supply networks. Care for the environment is one example I have already mentioned with regard to Wal-Mart. Workplace safety and material handling approaches are other examples.

Often these processes are enabled by systems that extend across the supply network. In the case of inventory and production management processes, the systems are transactional and model based. In the case of quality, safety, and environmental care, they are more likely to be principle and example based. The learning layer can complement these supply network systems by enabling process participants throughout the network to learn from one another. Examples that are most relevant can be suggested by the system. Experts from other organizations can be suggested as required. The Supply Network Architect can decide the degree to which knowledge in the learning layer is shared among members of the supply network. It can be orchestrated as a hub-and-spoke model if competitive relationships among suppliers dictate. In other cases, a greater degree of learning transparency among network participants may be feasible and desirable.

Supply Network Architects typically have a significant number of suppliers of *know-how*, such as engineering, IT, management consulting, investment banking, and legal services, and the learning layer can be applied to amplify the value of the intellectual capital for which these types of suppliers are being paid. A shared learning layer can be made a *standard delivery mechanism* of these suppliers' deliverables, as well as providing a means for enhanced access to the experts associated with the deliverables. This model shifts the relationship from episodic engagements, in which the deliverables often gather dust, or are not assimilated by any but a small portion of the receiving organization, to a model of continuous and efficient transfer of intellectual capital.

Supply Network Architects are often acquisitive by nature since they rely on being well positioned in the value chain, and acquisitions (and more rarely, mergers) are a means to adjust their position as required. The learning layer facilitates acquisitions that will be successful over the long term by more rapidly and continuously transferring knowledge and learning among acquiring and acquired organization. By virtue of the learning layer doing the suggesting of contacts and experts, it serves to more quickly break down barriers to communication by reducing the hesitancy to reach out when appropriate.

Adaptive process networks can be used to gracefully synthesize the best of the processes of the acquiring and acquired organizations, resulting in a new process that is better than the predecessor processes, and with built-in transitioning and change management features. The learning layer enables the capture of process and intellectual capital synergies that have previously proved elusive in so many acquisitions. When an acquisition occurs, the business fabric of two different organizations has to be woven together. The learning layer can take the ragged, hand stitching of the executive teams and consultants that put the combined organization together, and over time create a seamless tapestry that is stronger than either of the original fabrics.

As an example, it can often take years for a newly combined organization to transition people to their ultimate physical locations, and perhaps even longer to fully integrate or replace systems that are not fully compatible. The learning layer can provide a rapid overlay that creates a "good enough" short-term integration. Then, as people use the learning layer, contribute new knowledge, and make more linkages with existing knowledge, the learning layer will begin to adapt accordingly and knit the organization ever closer together.

So in summary, for the Supply Network Architect, whose success rests on maximally generating value from the operational synergy among their organizations, as well as capturing value from the business ecosystem around them, the learning layer enables wringing out the next level of value generation that is possible with this business model. It enables more efficient, effective, and scalable coordination and transfer of learning internally, and serves as a platform for the business to better establish its processes throughout the business ecosystem. And it enables more effective capture, amplification, and assimilation of intellectual capital from its professional service providers.

Relationship Owners

Let us now explore some applications of the learning layer that are more typically associated with businesses or organizations that are closer to the province of the Relationship Owner model (figure 14.2). Regardless of your organization's specific position on our tapestry, you are most likely going to be intensely interested in enhancing your customer relationships. This nearly universal interest is reflected in a recent survey of business executives by Forrester Research that found that the executives' *number one* priority for new investments in IT was acquiring and retaining customers.[1]

For knowledge-based businesses whose revenues are based on *delivering their expertise* to customers, extending the learning layer into their clients' organizations represents an exciting new opportunity for establishing and sustaining valuable client relationships. I've witnessed several powerful examples of this with early versions of learning layers.

For instance, one of the world's largest business and IT consultancies was pursuing a master service agreement

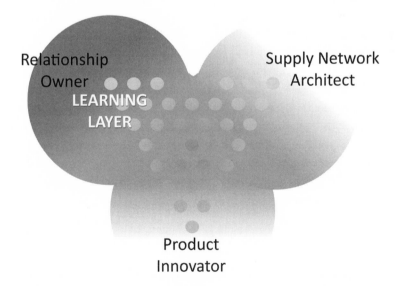

Figure 14.2 Building Learning into the Fabric of Relationship Owners

opportunity with a Fortune top 20 company that had the potential to be worth upwards of $200 million per year. Large consultancies are the quintessential Relationship Owners—they seek to achieve privileged relationships with client executives, and sell wide-ranging, long-term solutions to their organizations. This consultancy was facing a situation in which there were already two formidable incumbents servicing the account, while they had negligible presence in the prospective client organization, and by their own admission could credibly demonstrate little in the way of differentiated products and services versus the incumbents.

Frankly, when they reviewed the situation with me and ManyWorlds colleagues, I thought the situation was a lost cause. I suspected their prospective client was just stringing them along to use as a negotiating chip to drive a better deal with the incumbents. But to strengthen their pretty weak hand, they licensed our technology and asked us to help put together a simple version of an online learning network that could be extended to the prospective client, serving to demonstrate a strong commitment and capability to transfer intellectual capital to the client on a continuing basis.

A significant amount of the consultancy's content was loaded into the network, along with profiles of their relevant experts, and even courseware for training programs that were normally for internal use only. The prospective client was invited to kick the tires on the learning network for a few weeks. Then the pursuit culminated in the managing director of the consultancy giving her final pitch presentation directly from the online learning network environment, and demonstrating some its key features to the prospective client's executive committee in real time. Lo and behold, it worked! The clients were impressed by the unique approach and the consultancy clinched the deal—actually displacing one of the entrenched incumbents!

I also witnessed something similar in more of a David and Goliath situation in which a boutique consultancy was up against a couple of the world's largest consulting organizations for a strategy engagement with a major retailer. To demonstrate unique capabilities, the boutique firm built a learning network environment that would serve to support engagement deliverables and facilitate collaborative learning. They too actually conducted their proposal presentation directly from the online learning network. And they too were successful in winning the client.

Both of these highly successful learning network applications happened to be motivated and driven by the supply side of a professional services relationship. But the collaborative learning network concept can also be driven by the demand side. I emphasized this point with regard to Supply Network Architects, but *every* client has a strong incentive to ensure the most efficient and sustainable transfer of learning as possible from their suppliers of intellectual capital. A collaborative learning layer should be a mandatory element of any knowledge-based relationship!

Recall that one of the core value drivers for Relationship Owners is managing the demand chain. This amounts to working backwards from the customer to orchestrate a network of supply. But increasingly in today's economy, it means actually *developing* innovative solutions that the current supply network cannot readily deliver. Once again, our flipping-the-funnel and associated capability component management approach can be applied.

We saw that for the Product Innovator, the application of flipping the funnel was about product or service level innovation, whereas for the Supply Network Architect the application was more typically with regard to project, process and venture development and management. The Relationship Owner will leverage the innovation aspects of flipping the funnel similarly to the Product Innovator, while also leveraging the network architecture aspects similarly to the Supply Network Architect. The difference is that for the Relationship Owner there will be an increasing emphasis on working backwards from *specific customer* unfulfilled needs rather than overall marketplace needs, and the innovation will be more likely to constitute a *solution*, where the solution is a bundle of products and services, some or all which will be sourced through a demand chain.

So as in the case of the Product Innovators and Supply Network Architects, the learning layer can help support value-driven, combinatorial-based innovation by managing an array of capability components and associated knowledge assets and social networks. But what is particularly exciting about the learning layer opportunity for Relationship Owners is that the solution development and flipping-the-funnel process can be extended right into the customer organization. In other words, the learning layer itself can help to serve as the conduit of solution ideas against which the capability network can be applied. In some cases the solution ideas may directly originate with the client, and the learning layer environment serves to ensure these ideas find their way to the right people at the right time. In other cases, the ideas may stem from insights *inferred* from patterns of behaviors associated with the customer. The Relationship Owner that applies the learning layer in this way will in a sense increasingly *merge* its innovation and operational processes with those of its customers, a situation that becomes the ultimate in privileged relationships.

Consumer-facing Applications

The predominant focus of this book has been the learning layer applied *within* an organization, with extensions to other customer and supplier *organizations*. In the somewhat dated jargon of Internet applications, these can be considered business-to-employee (B2E) and business-to-business (B2B) applications. But obviously learning systems will also have a transformational impact on business-to-consumer (B2C) applications. B2C applications include standard e-commerce applications in which products are sold to customers, but also include applications of a community-building nature, in which the value generated is less direct than as is the case for standard e-commerce.

For example, today we can be a fan on Facebook of our favorite grocery stores, restaurants and auto shops, not just of Hollywood movie stars. Procter and Gamble's many communities help us to "love our laundry and delight our senses" by allowing us to provide online suggestions on the development of their new household cleaner, while also helping us better care for our pets' nutritional needs and the wrinkles on our skin. Specific groups can be targeted, such as mothers of small children who enjoy sharing novel and often humorous uses of existing products; or even those who love their Sharpie pens enough to want to share tips on use and demonstrate their own creativity (and loyalty!). This collaborative conversation by design allows us as a consumer to participate in developing the products we will ultimately buy. Relationship Owners can capitalize on this collaboration even more, by enabling discussion and feedback across a *range* of products, all the while "listening" for unfulfilled needs. In these cases, the learning layer can foster the knitting together of communities that deliver additional consumers, members, and advertising recipients; or serve to provide valuable information to network members.

For standard e-commerce applications, the learning layer simply represents the culmination of the historical trend. The most advanced of the automatic recommendation systems have already proved their worth in e-commerce—they clearly drive additional revenues. It has been reported, for example, that Amazon attributes upwards of 35 percent of their sales to recommendations—a truly colossal impact![2] And the next generation of e-commerce characterized by adaptive recommendations, including not only unprompted recommendations, but also variations such as personalized search and behavioral-based advertising are becoming prevalent. Adding to these capabilities adaptive social networking features, and navigation structures that automatically adapt to users, promises to deliver even more value to consumers. The e-commerce trend toward the learning layer is inevitable and accelerating.

A distinguishing feature in implementing consumer-based e-commerce learning networks is that e-commerce applications will typically have *purchase patterns* with which to work that will not be available in most internal business applications. Since the more behavioral information that is available, the better, this is an advantage for e-commerce systems. On the other hand, standard e-commerce applications will tend to be disadvantaged versus knowledge worker learning layer applications in that they will typically be accessed by any particular user much less frequently, and therefore have a proportionally less rich set of *non-transactional* information from which to base inferences.

Of course, e-commerce players will naturally try to make up for this disadvantage—the hunger for access to a richer set of behavioral information is the reason the major commercial Internet players are attempting to increase their scope as much as possible. They want to learn as much about you as possible, and access to more behavioral data associated with a greater variety of behaviors is the path to better learning. This is just a corollary to the Relationship Owner value driver of optimizing relationship scope. We normally would think of that in the context of scope of *products and services*, but here we see the value driver has an analog with regard to the *scope of learning* associated with the customer.

Regardless of the differences in data sets available, adaptive recommendations will surely become a dominant form of interface on e-commerce sites. When coupled with intelligent, credible *explanations* of the recommendations, the relationship with the customer becomes increasingly intimate and trending toward exclusivity. And the opportunity is not just recommending specific products—the learning layer can recommend other customers who may be able to share relevant experiences, thereby strongly facilitating the sense of customer community that is so rewarding to both the customers and the merchant.

In fact, the learning layer extended to consumers will enable businesses to more quickly and effectively tune their strategies and tactics than was previously possible by providing a richer set of consumer behavior information. I mentioned earlier that some recommendations may constitute experiments, where the system probes the boundaries of the recommendation recipients' interests and preferences. More broadly, *all* recommendations and the subsequent behaviors of recommendation recipients can be thought of as a set of ongoing experiments. As we saw earlier, every business activity has two sources of value: a direct value and an expected learning value. So it is with adaptive recommendations; even if a recommendation is not meant to explicitly be an experiment, it will always have some by-product informational value—or in other words, some expected learning value.

By analyzing aggregates of these recommendation experiments, patterns can be discerned that provide valuable insights. For example, customer *segments* may emerge that would otherwise remain hidden in the transactional background noise. Or correlations may be uncovered among products that would on the surface not be expected to have anything in common. These data-driven insights can be applied to adjust marketing tactics appropriately and tune pricing. Certainly, some of this is already done in advanced e-commerce sites—it is just that the degree of resolution of the insights will become increasingly fine grained, and the system itself will be able to automatically take appropriate actions on the basis of these insights. This is an automated culmination of a general trend that Erik Brynjolfsson and Michael Schrage have emphasized is already having profound productivity implications—the acceleration of innovation that is made possible by the ability to conduct timelier, as well as cheaper, experiments.[3]

At the strategic level, Relationship Owners always seek to optimize their scope of products and services to a customer. That means they want to increase their scope as much as possible, but not so far that their relationship ends up becoming diluted. Tesco, the UK-based supermarket giant is a good example of this. Tesco has been expanding from a basic supermarket to a Relationship Owner—a retail solution provider. This includes services very far afield from foodstuffs—for example, providing financial services such as mortgages and insurance and providing its customers the ability to compare electricity and gas prices. The common theme is to offer great value to the consumer, and then build on the familiarity and comfort of everyday needs to continuously expand the share of the consumer's spend. To optimize scope successfully, and efficiently, companies like Tesco have to run physical experiments—they have to try things, and then run with them if they turn out to be profitable or fold them up if they appear to not be able to get to sustained profitability. The learning layer will provide the auxiliary level of insights from virtual interactions to help ensure scope is optimized at the lowest possible cost to the business.

Corporate Functions

Let's now wrap-up our tour of the business model tapestry by reviewing some applications of the learning layer that are equally relevant to just about every business, regardless of their position on our tapestry. Many of such applications will reside with *corporate functions,* including Corporate Strategy, Finance, IT, and HR (figure 14.3).

Corporate Strategy and Analysis Functions

Business renewal *management* processes such as strategy and business portfolio management are clear candidates for the benefits of the learning layer. These are data, knowledge, modeling and presentation-intense areas in which there is often a good deal of reinvention because it can be difficult to find relevant historical material rapidly enough. Transforming ongoing deliverables and work products from internal and third party analysts and consultants into knowledge assets within a learning layer can make these processes much more efficient and effective. Similarly, business and competitor intelligence are related processes that can benefit from

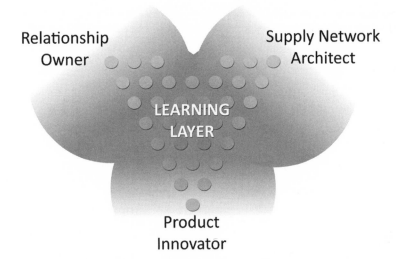

Relationship Owner

Supply Network Architect

LEARNING LAYER

Product Innovator

Figure 14.3 Building Learning into the Fabric of Corporate Functions

a learning layer implementation. These are often very data-intense functions, but if they are relegated to just exercises in ad hoc searching and data mining, learning is not effectively institutionalized. The learning layer can transform what would otherwise be just a vast collection of facts and figures into a true web of learning.

As an example, I was recently discussing a competitor intelligence application for a large company. This company wanted to piece together disparate types of information, and leverage a network of contributors of publicly available information. The contributors would include employees attending conferences and other events, and non-employees, including academic institutions and other third parties. The company had found that they were unable to successfully handle this seemingly fairly simple system with their current content management systems. It was just too hard to try to repurpose existing information residing in these traditional content systems for the competitor intelligence application, and the content systems were too unwieldy to conveniently extend to employees and others in the field who might uncover relevant information. The obvious solution was to establish a learning layer on top of the existing content and systems, integrating data and content as required into the layer's network without disturbing the underlying systems, and then extend the learning layer so that it could be easily accessed by people in the field.

Finance

Similar to the corporate strategy function, the Finance function is by nature a data-intensive and knowledge-intensive set of interlocking processes. So there is an obvious fit for the learning layer. But Finance also has accountability for extending standard financial processes throughout the business. With its ability to generate automatic metrics associated with process use, the learning layer can provide the information needed for the Finance function to understand what's working well with these distributed financial processes, and what needs adjustment.

In addition, the learning layer facilitates the generation of metrics that enable the quantifications of learning in way never before possible. This provides Finance the means to effectively package the quantifications in *financial terms* for use by management and stakeholders, facilitating Finance in playing a more meaningful role in directly assisting in the management of the business's intellectual capital growth.

IT Organization

Once again, as an organization comprised of knowledge workers, the learning layer will deliver direct benefits to the IT organization by enhancing its internal learning. But it can do much more for the IT function. IT has overall accountability for effectively managing knowledge assets. But as a former CIO, I know full well that historically there has been little visibility with regard to the value that various knowl-edge assets actually deliver to the business. For example, I have seen cases in which large-scale, costly intranets were established, and post-implementation it was not apparent which parts were providing significant value and which parts were underutilized. Sure, some basic site metrics such as the number of page views were available. But those metrics were too coarse grained to provide the guidance required for optimization.

The learning layer can provide the fine-grained metrics, down to the individual knowledge assets, required for IT to make informed operational and investment decisions. Not just providing basic page view data, but generating a rich set of meaningful information, including the amount of influence, or learning power, individual and collections of knowledge assets deliver. This enables IT to make effective development and maintenance decisions firmly grounded on current, value-driven information. Even better, the learning layer can assist in managing the entire network of knowledge assets by automatically adjusting network relationships and structures on the basis of its sophisticated inferences from behavioral information. This provides the detailed level of adaptation that would simply be prohibitively expensive to do manually.

The learning layer can also serve to revitalize existing applications. Often as the business changes, applications are discarded and replaced. This occurs even if, say, 80 percent of the existing application remains useful. The monolithic nature of these applications makes an 80 percent solution not good enough for most users, because the 20 percent that is obsolete becomes too much of a hassle to deal with. By apply-ing the learning layer over the top of these applications, the useful 80 percent can be retained and exposed to users, while the other 20 percent is gracefully replaced with up-to-date modules. The days of massive IT implementations and then massive replacements before the investment is even recouped is coming to a close!

Human Resources

The Human Resources organization represents a treasure trove of opportunities for which to apply the learning layer. Most fundamentally, the learning layer can help manage activities throughout the entire *employee lifecycle*.

Of course, in today's world, even the concept of *employee* becomes increasingly tenuous. Much has been made of the company of one concept, the freelance nation, and so on. Perhaps the more general notion is simply that business has become *fuzzier*. Certainly, there are legal constructs that have to necessarily be more black and white, but from a practical standpoint increasingly the boundaries of the business are blurred. There are, for example, full-time employees, part-time employees, joint ventures, independent contractors on long-term engagements, and short-term contractors. We have run headlong into shades of gray again. Call them collectively *fuzzy employees*. And where we have fuzzy employees, we need fuzzy networks, and that means we need the learning layer because it uniquely can provide the flexibility to adapt to the fuzzy boundaries as they shift over time.

That (fuzzy) employee lifecycle starts with recruiting, and the learning layer can serve as a social and knowledge network that automatically begins establishing your relationship with prospective employees. In interacting with your learning layer, a prospective employee can receive automatic recommendations of relevant information and relevant people with whom to talk. The learning layer can enable prospective employees to creatively assemble and update a *network* of information for you to assess rather than just a sending a sterile resume. And from a generational standpoint, college recruits have grown up in a world of Web 2.0 capabilities, and they will expect at least that, and probably more, from your company.

At an additional level of sophistication, the *capability component network* concept can be leveraged to assist in the recruiting process. Specific human resource needs can be identified in the enterprise's or business unit's capability network on an ongoing basis. These needs can then be matched against the networks of information provided by prospective resources. Automatic recommendations can be generated that highlight good fits directly to line management or HR as desired. Compare this with just sifting through resumes and then essentially hiring in bulk and seeing who sticks.

Once hired, the next phase of the lifecycle is employee *onboarding*, in which, again, the "employee" may be any of the relationship shades of gray up to and including the traditional full-time employee. Most companies these days already have a pretty effective onboarding process in place, and have assembled online resources through which the newly hired can conveniently access the basic information required to become an effective member of the organization. What the learning layer can deliver in addition to these basics is the ability for the new hire to more quickly tap into the collective wisdom of the organization—to get the knowledge that is most relevant to his particular job given his particular experience level, and to quickly connect with people that are likely to be most helpful to him during his initial time at the company. Early on, he may not even know to ask some of the questions that are most relevant and important, much less whom to ask, and no canned set of "frequently asked questions" is likely to completely hit the mark. The learning layer may be able to make a useful suggestion it derives from the experience of others long before the new hire realizes there is a question to be asked.

And again, if the new hire is a college recruit, she is going to expect at least as sophisticated a set of capabilities as found on Internet sites she frequents. She will definitely not be impressed with legacy content management systems and HTML pages! A bad experience during onboarding can lead to early disillusionment. This is not an exaggeration—I have heard this directly from young recruits at major corporations who have been flabbergasted at the difference between what they have been used to on the Internet and the internal corporate systems they now must use. It is important to recognize the anomaly of the past few years—it is really the first time in the history of IT in which the capabilities available to the general public are often more sophisticated than what is available within corporations. Historically, it was very much the opposite. The learning layer can serve to reverse the situation back to the historical norm!

Once beyond the onboarding phase, education and training becomes an ongoing process, and an increasingly important one in today's fast paced and rapidly changing world. Ongoing corporate education represents one of the greatest opportunities for the learning layer. Today, the management of corporate education and training programs has become quite sophisticated. For example, learning management systems (LMS) may be used to manage education programs for each employee over time. The LMS includes courses available, what courses the employee has completed, and the courses that the employee is scheduled to take and when. In addition, many corporate education programs include online courses, and multimedia-based training is routinely delivered to employees and contractors. What has been missing is the glue to integrate all of this into an adaptive environment—an environment, for example, in which feedback about specific courses, or people's experiences of applying the content of the courses in the workplace, is integrated and easily available to others.

But that's just table stakes. What is really needed is a *real-time learning* environment. There will always be a need for episodic training programs, and the existing corporate processes generally do a pretty good job at that. But what they don't do is deliver learning in real time, when the employee most needs it. That wasn't technically feasible previously. But the learning layer can make that happen. In fact, it can vastly amplify the value of the existing corporate education process and materials. By simply converting the education materials into knowledge assets, and embedding them into the learning layer, we get an adaptive education environment. The educational assets become more valuable by virtue of having an adaptive social network wrapped around them.

With this approach, rather than being a standalone process, corporate education effectively merges with the learning layer. Specific educational assets, feedback on the assets, and people associated with the assets, can all be intelligently recommended by the system when people need them in the course of their particular work activities. In fact, the educational assets can easily be connected to specific *process steps*, and recommended by the system appropriately. The learning layer becomes that adaptive cockpit, with educational assets and other learning being automatically suggested as appropriate, along with explanations of why they were suggested, as you maneuver through your daily work. And your maneuvers in turn help to effortlessly build the base of learning that others can then benefit from.

Inevitably employees leave the company. It used to be that occurred most typically at retirement, but for most businesses these days it will generally occur well before the employee is due a gold watch. Regardless of when and how employees leave, the risk of the past has been that learning would inevitably and irrevocably be lost. The learning layer is really the first practical solution to reducing the risk of learning loss as the workforce turns over. Not only do the employees' documents remain, but something much more important also remains—the learning that occurred during the course of their work is retained within the learning layer, continuing to provide value to others long after they have moved on.

PART IV

BUILDING LEARNING INTO THE FABRIC OF *YOUR* BUSINESS

15

Implementing the Learning Layer

Our journey from the very basics of how the brain learns to socially aware systems to evolving learning networks to adaptive business processes and to application areas tuned to an organization's specific fabric has hopefully established for you the value, as well as the inevitability, of systems and processes that can actually learn and maintain themselves embedded throughout the enterprise. It is not just a promise of the future—the fundamental capabilities can be a reality right now in any organization. And as we have all experienced to our regret, learning is ephemeral—every day that goes by in which learning is not captured in an organization is learning that is lost forever. So this naturally leads to the question of how can you begin to take advantage of this next wave of technology-enabled business improvement within *your* organization?

Aristotle may not have gotten it quite right about the fuzziness of the world, but he did have the sage and sensible advice of "moderation in all things." So it is with implementing the learning layer. Even though an implementation can be remarkably simple and has minimal risk given the learning layer's complementarity with existing systems, as with any new paradigm, it makes sense to move conservatively until you have gained some experience. Given positive results from your initial moves, it will then be the time to move more aggressively, particularly when a competitive advantage is at stake. So with that in mind, following is a very general set of steps (yes, a process!) to consider in implementing a learning layer in your organization.

Determine Potential Application Areas

There are two particularly compelling targets for an initial learning layer implementation: either an area in which something is broken and a learning layer could offer a good shot at providing the fix or an area in which things have been going pretty well, but achieving the next level of performance will likely require the capabilities of a learning layer.

To identify candidates of the first type, a good way to start is to take a look across your organization and identify the areas for which there is much in the way of knowledge and expertise, but dissatisfaction with the ability to take advantage of this intellectual capital, or in which any semblance of process is missing in action. For most organizations, areas in which knowledge workers predominate, such as technology development and support, R&D, head office functions, and marketing and sales, are prime targets.

For candidate implementation areas of the second type, the business fabric framework and associated learning layer example applications we covered earlier in the book can be helpful. Take some time to think about where your business (or organization within your business) is positioned on the tapestry, where you want to be, which value drivers are most emphasized given your current position, and how that emphasis might shift. Then scan your current systems and processes and evaluate their ability to ensure that you will be clearly better than your competition for the value drivers that will matter most to you. If there are some cases in which these value drivers will not be sufficiently superior, then those are areas that may be good candidates for a learning layer implementation.

I've found that processes (whether officially designated as such or not) that *span* organizations can be excellent candidates for initial learning layer implementations, including client-facing applications. Some examples that we covered earlier include multi-organization processes that support innovation or product development, or situations in which a professional services-based business wants to collaboratively extend its intellectual capital delivery processes directly into client organizations.

Prioritize Candidate Pilots and Select

After you have identified some candidate learning layer application areas, you should conduct an evaluation of each of these areas on the basis of the criticality of need, willingness of the community to do something about the need, and sufficiency of scale to attain effective results.

The criterion of criticality of need may be a function of the community dissatisfaction with the current environment or may be driven more by strategic or competitive concerns. In some organizations, a demographic factor may be the burning platform that needs to be addressed quickly—if a good portion of the expertise of an organization is tied up in workers who may leave the organization in the next few years, attempting to institutionalize this valuable base of learning before it is lost will be an imperative.

It is generally pretty easy to find communities willing to do something about a critical need, as long as it is not disruptive of their normal work activities. And since the learning layer is not at all disruptive, and learns without any special effort on the part of participants, it most likely will be very welcome. So it would be most unusual that a candidate area is disqualified on this ground, but you may want to avoid an initial implementation with a group of hard-core curmudgeons—you can always pick them up later.

With regard to the criterion of sufficient scale, candidate areas that comprise less than a dozen or so active participants should be deferred or combined with other areas. Since the learning layer derives its learning from people, the more people the better. At least several dozen active participants make for the best pilots.

I suggest you prioritize the candidate areas on the basis of the evaluation criteria, and select one or two of the candidate areas to serve as the initial pilots. With the pilot area(s) selected, you can establish a simple implementation plan (simple because there generally isn't much required) and some criteria for evaluating the results of the pilot. Example evaluation criteria of pilot results include the level of participation in contributing new knowledge assets and creating new topics, the perceived value-add of the recommendations and other adaptive communications to users, and the overall reduction in time spent in accessing information to support the participants' work activities. If it is a client facing application, you would want to include criteria on the degree of improvement in your client relationship.

Initialize the Learning Layer

The knowledge assets (e.g., documents, models, intranet applications, Internet-based resources, etc.) that are frequently used by members of the pilot organization should be evaluated to determine what should be integrated into an initial learning layer. It is best to have a minimum of a few hundred knowledge assets incorporated into the learning layer at start-up. There is no upper bound—it could be many thousands of knowledge assets—the more the better from a learning perspective.

The initial set of knowledge assets may be established on a first-cut basis by enterprise search engine technology that builds a rough taxonomy. Or other types of utilities may be used to help translate identified sets of information and documents into knowledge assets within the learning layer by intelligently extracting descriptive information where it is available. This descriptive information can then be automatically loaded into the learning layer, which will then apply it to the appropriate knowledge object. Some manual effort will typically be required in establishing, or at least tuning, a starter set of topical areas for the pilot and building some relationships among the topics and the knowledge assets. Depending on the application area, you may choose to add some process sequences to the learning layer as well, or that can come later.

It will usually be worthwhile to keep the learning layer "light weight" by just having it primarily *reference* existing information and systems. This allows you to keep using your underlying existing systems to do what they do best, with the learning layer just adding value by complementing your existing system portfolio rather than replacing or duplicating anything.

Once this starter-set learning layer is in place, you are ready to let the users loose on it, and the learning layer will then bootstrap itself from there! The users can quickly add and customize their social networking profiles, create their own topical areas of interest, and add their own knowledge assets as desired. The system begins its learning immediately.

Evaluate the Results

You will be in a position to effectively evaluate the value-add of the learning layer against the evaluation criteria you established within a couple months of implementation. By that time the learning layer will have had enough user activity to have effectively learned preferences and interests, and to make some self-modifications. Follow-up assessments can be conducted every couple of months thereafter.

This is also a time to highlight the contributions of pilot participants. The positive reinforcement that comes from highlighting their contributions to organizational learning is automatically and continuously performed by the learning layer itself, but this information can beneficially be more widely disseminated throughout the organization. A participant's level of *influence* as calculated by the learning layer is a good, general purpose indicator of the learning value a participant is generating and is therefore a particularly good metric to broadcast. The amount of content authored, or more generally contributed to the learning network, is also a metric worthy of highlighting.

Extend the Learning Layer

As the learning layer proves itself in the initial pilots, you can extend it to other candidate areas of your organization. This is a very simple and natural process—more participants are added and the learning layer just encompasses additional legacy knowledge assets as required. The beauty is that as the scope of implementation increases, the value-add to your organization will increase more than linearly due to both the inherent increasing returns to scale of the network and the learning effects of the layer. Intellectual capital acceleration will become a reality for your organization!

For large-scale adaptive process implementations, or for very large-scale incorporation of existing knowledge bases into the learning layer, external solution providers may be able to provide auxiliary capabilities if resources within your organization are constrained. But no programming whatsoever should be required to implement any of the basic features discussed in this book, so it is more a matter of internal resource constraints rather than required skills that is the determining factor on the use of external capabilities.

That's really all there is to implementing a learning layer throughout your organization. In the very unlikely event you ever wanted to un-implement, it is just a matter of deleting in a few seconds the web of relationships, behavioral information, and inferencing capabilities that comprises the learning layer. This leaves untouched all of the data and systems on which it rested. The learning layer truly is robust yet ethereal in nature.

So whether your emphasis is on enhanced support of your knowledge workers or to more intelligently serve your customers, it starts with learning. Kick start some pilots and take the first step toward a stronger, but more flexible, business fabric spun from the loom of the learning layer!

16

Conclusion

We have taken our journey. We touched on how the brain learns by modifying its underlying structure, and how it evolved its power by adding new layers of richly connected networks. We found that we can employ a similar fuzzy network structure to enable our systems to adapt. Our systems can also be made to pay attention to us—they can become socially aware. They can then provide us useful adaptive recommendations of many forms and in many contexts. They can even turn these recommendations back upon themselves and direct their own adaptation and evolution. Thus emerges our learning layer. And we can integrate our social networks and our processes directly within this learning layer. The learning layer is an "it" and yet it is *us*, and yet again, somehow *more* than just the sum of us. It is something of a nature that is totally new. The immediate opportunities and benefits are manifest, but as with anything that is different in kind, the ultimate possibilities and value will be discovered as we go along.

What we *can* be sure of is that with the learning layer we have a way to address that other half of the intellectual capital picture that has been so well hidden in plain sight (figure 16.1). Social awareness of our systems will allow us to tap the cognitive surplus that has been residing in our organizations all along. And our systems will infer and learn from this cognitive surplus, and generate valuable recommendations on the basis of this learning. Our work will be

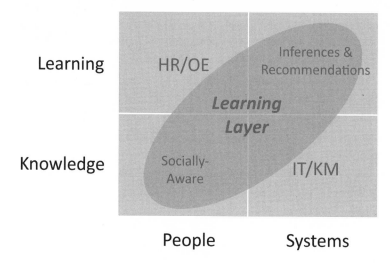

Figure 16.1 The Opportunity Fulfilled

the learning layer, and the learning layer will be our work. Our productivity will jump and our intellectual capital will accelerate.

Some aspects of our businesses will simply be improved by the learning layer; others will be completely transformed. We toured the various textures of the fabric that we find woven throughout our tapestry of business possibilities, and we highlighted selected opportunities for building learning right into this fabric. What we touched on were only the most obvious applications of the learning layer: business renewal applications such as R&D, business development processes, and innovation supported by the creative combinatorics of flipping the funnel; enhanced integration with customers and suppliers, project experience transfer, M&A support, strategy and business intelligence, and so on. Beyond these specific application areas, any knowledge-based organization or process will clearly benefit from the learning layer, and you will undoubtedly find many applications in your business that I have not imagined. Corporate education and training processes in general will surely ultimately merge with the learning layer, transforming to the personalized and the real-time.

The adaptive enterprise has been a dream for some time. But even if the corporate spirit was willing, the underlying fabric has just been too brittle. It was prone to tearing when pulled, and shattering when shifted, and so the reality was that businesses could not adapt as effectively as they needed to. So they didn't move much. They could see the punches coming, but they stood flat-footed, pinned against the ropes. The learning layer will build adaptation into your business's fabric—you'll have a better ability to bob and weave, to counter, and to dance across the canvas when you need to. But the learning layer delivers more than just adaptation and resilience—it will increase your business's regenerative powers, its powers of innovation, renewal, and revitalization. Learning that is built to last makes for a business that lasts as well.

This all sounds wonderful. And ultimately it will be. But it starts with a first step. The beauty is that the *implementation* of the learning layer is itself adaptable—not a monolithic, all or nothing, implementation. It can start small. It will complement existing systems and content, and make them more valuable to you. The learning layer can then grow and evolve at a pace that fits naturally for your business. If you start learning layers in different parts of your company, they will inevitably seek each other out and seamlessly merge. The metrics that are automatically generated by the learning layer will help guide the direction you want to take it. And at the end of the day, no matter what romantic sounding metaphors we apply to the learning layer, financial value rules. The learning layer obeys that understanding, and brings a value discipline to the vast areas of the business that have been previously hidden from it.

The journey we have taken is through a world that is for the most part all possible now. And the purpose of this book was to highlight the possibilities that are within the realm of the here and now, and within the context of your particular business. But I must admit that it has been very difficult to restrain myself regarding other future possibilities that are merely extensions—inevitable extensions—of the path we traveled here. Certainly the evolution of the Internet itself into the *one* learning layer to complement all others is an obvious inevitability, although the twists and turns to get there are hard to predict. And along the way there will develop what are essentially just basic extensions of the learning layer capabilities I have described of the here and now that will engender a new level of wonder, and deliver applications not yet conceived. Things like recommendations adapting to your specific location as you travel through a city. Things like media, such as videos and games, automatically adapting. Things like distributed learning layers syndicating and adaptively combining. And things like the explanation engine exhibiting a personality, and a personality that actually adapts over time. Perchance even to dream.

Had I the heavens' embroidered cloths,
Enwrought with golden and silver light,
The blue and the dim and the dark cloths
Of night and light and the half-light,
I would spread the cloths under your feet:
But I, being poor, have only my dreams;
I have spread my dreams under your feet;
Tread softly, because you tread on my dreams.
—William Butler Yeats

Notes

Chapter 1

1. See Albert-Laszlo Barabasi, "Scale-Free Networks: A Decade and Beyond" *Science* 325 (July 24, 2009): 412–413 for an overview of how the network paradigm has influenced scientific fields over the past decade.
2. James Surowiecki, *The Wisdom of Crowds: Why the Many Are Smarter Than the Few and How Collective Wisdom Shapes Business, Economies, Societies and Nations* (New York: Doubleday, 2004).
3. Michael Chui, Andy Miller, and Roger P. Roberts, "Six Ways to Make Web 2.0 Work" *McKinsey Quarterly*, February 2009.

Chapter 2

1. Lowell L. Bryan and Claudia I. Joyce, *Mobilizing Minds: Creating Wealth from Talent in the 21st-Century Organization* (New York: McGraw-Hill, 2007).
2. John Hagel III, John Seely Brown, and Lang Davison, "The Big Shift: Measuring the Forces of Change" *Harvard Business Review* (July-August, 2009): 86–89.
3. Jack Welch, "A Learning Company and Its Quest for Six Sigma." Speech given at 1997 General Electric Corporation's Annual Shareholder Meeting. http://web.archive.org/web/20010124085100/http://www.ge.com/news/welch/speeches/sigma.htm.
4. David A. Garvin, *Learning in Action: A Guide to Putting the Learning Organization to Work* (Boston: Harvard Business School Press, 2000).
5. Adapted from Steven Flinn, "The Math of Learning." *www.manyworlds.com* (February 7, 2004).

6. Clay Shirky, "Gin, Television, and Social Surplus." *www.shirky.com* (April 26, 2008).

Chapter 3

1. Some higher-level structures or processes of the brain may be organized, at least as a first approximation, hierarchically. For example, see Jeff Hawkins and Sandra Blakeslee, *On Intelligence* (New York: Times Books, 2004), for a compelling exposition of a hypothesis concerning hierarchy-based structures and processes of the neocortex. Nevertheless, the brain's most fundamental topology is that of a network.
2. Roozbeh Kiani and Michael Shadlen, "Representation of Confidence Associated with a Decision by Neurons in the Parietal Cortex" *Science* 324 (May 8, 2009): 759–764.
3. See, for example, Greg Miller's review "Sleeping to Reset Overstimulated Synapses" *Science* 324 (April 3, 2009): 22.
4. Andrew N. Meltzoff et al., "Foundations for a New Science of Learning" *Science* 325 (July 17, 2009): 284.
5. See Clara Moskowitz, "Teen Brains Clear Out Childhood Thoughts" *www.livescience.com* (March 23, 2009), which includes relevant comments from Ian Campbell of the University of California, Davis, on his research.
6. Damien Fair et al., "Functional Brain Networks Develop From a 'Local to Distributed' Organization" *PLOS Computational Biology* 5 no. 5 (May 2009): 1–14.
7. Moskowitz, "Teen Brains Clear Out Childhood Thoughts."

Chapter 4

1. See Bart Kosko, *Fuzzy Thinking: The New Science of Fuzzy Logic* (New York: Hyperion, 1993) for a good background on the general topic of "fuzziness." Kosko does a marvelous job of explaining fuzzy sets and logic, along with extensions of the mathematics to a variety of real-world implications and applications. He uses Aristotle as a foil, and I follow his lead, although perhaps a bit more tongue in cheek.

Chapter 5

1. The description of this experiment is adapted from Vanessa Woods and Brian Hare, *www.edge.org* edition 294 (July 16, 2009).
2. See Kiyoshi Nakahara and Yasushi Miyashita, "Understanding Intentions: Through the Looking Glass" *Science* 308 (April 29, 2005): 644–645, for a summary of the role of mirror neurons. Autism, for example, which comprises a spectrum of disorders, is characterized by various degrees of limitation in the ability to process the behavioral cues of others. There is some evidence that a contributing factor may be a dysfunction of the mirror neuron system. See Lindsay M. Oberman et al., "EEG Evidence for Mirror Neuron Dysfunction in Autism Spectrum Disorders" *Cognitive Brain Research* 24 (July 2005): 190–198. More recent studies suggest that various neuronal communication issues may be an even more important causative factor with regard to autism spectrum disorders.
3. *CIO* (May 15, 2009): 15.

Chapter 6

1. *Fortune Brainstorm: TECH Conference*, Pasadena, CA: July 2009.

Chapter 8

1. See Robin Dunbar, *Grooming, Gossip, and the Evolution of Language* (Cambridge, MA: Harvard University Press, 1998) and Malcolm Gladwell, *The Tipping Point: How Little Things Make a Big Difference* (New York: Little, Brown and Company, 2000) pages 177–182.
2. See pages 218–219 in Lowell L. Bryan and Claudia I. Joyce, *Mobilizing Minds: Creating Wealth from Talent in the 21st⁻Century Organization* (New York: McGraw-Hill, 2007).

Chapter 9

1. John Hagel III, John Seely Brown, and Lang Davison, "The Big Shift: Measuring the Forces of Change" *Harvard Business Review* (July-August 2009): 87.

Chapter 10

1. The business fabric framework is an adaptation from, and an extension of, the ManyWorlds white paper "StrategySpace" *www.manyworlds.com*, January 2001. A sampling of the great number of earlier business strategy models and approaches that has informed the business fabric framework summarized in this book includes the pioneering works of Michael E. Porter: *Competitive Strategy: Creating and Sustaining Superior Performance* (New York: The Free Press, 1980) and *Competitive Advantage: Techniques for Analyzing Industries and Competitors* (New York: The Free Press, 1985); Michael Treacy and Fred Wiersema, *The Discipline of Market Leaders: Choose Your Customers, Narrow Your Focus, Dominate Your Market* (Reading, MA: Addison-Wesley, 1995); and John Hagel and Marc Singer, "Unbundling the Corporation" *Harvard Business Review* (March-April, 1999). For an excellent business strategy "meta-analysis" that categorizes and provides perspectives on the many approaches to business strategy, see Henry Mintzberg, Bruce Ahlstrand, and Joseph Lampel, *Strategy Safari: A Guided Your Through the Wilds of Strategic Management* (New York: The Free Press, 1998).
2. Sarah Lacy, "Amazon Buys Zappos" *www.techcrunch.com* (July 22, 2009).
3. Miguel Bustillo, "Wal-Mart to Assign New 'Green' Ratings" *Wall Street Journal* (July 16, 2009).

Chapter 11

1. "The State of the CIO '09: The Survey" *CIO* (January 1, 2009): 56.

Chapter 12

1. For an excellent expansion on, and for many examples of, the concept of innovation being fundamentally a process of combinatorial-based creativity, see Andrew Hargadon and Robert Sutton, "Building an Innovation Factory" *Harvard Business Review* (May-June 2000): 157–166 and Andrew Hargadon, *How Breakthroughs Happen: The Surprising Truth about How Companies Innovate* (Boston: Harvard Business School Publishing, 2003).

2. See Paul Rabinow, *Making PCR: A Story of Biotechnology* (University of Chicago Press, 1997) for an overview of PCR. Mullis's quote is on pages 6–7, and is originally from an account Mullis gave to the Smithsonian Institution.

3. This process for innovation and renewal was described in its basic form and is adapted from Steven Flinn, "Flipping the Funnel" *www.manyworlds.com*, June 2002.

Chapter 13

1. Harris Collingwood and Diane L. Coutu, "Jack on Jack: The HBR Interview" *Harvard Business Review* (February 2002): 93.

2. See, for example, Genrich Altshuller, *The Innovation Algorithm: TRIZ, Systematic Innovation and Technical Creativity* (Worcester, MA: Technical Innovation Center, Inc. 1999).

3. Jack Welch quote is from an interview of Welch by Elliott Masie at the "TechLearn 2001" conference in Orlando, FL (October 29, 2001).

4. Steven Pinker, *The Language Instinct* (New York: Harper-Collins, 1995). See pages 75–78 for the initial description of discrete combinatorial processes.

Chapter 14

1. From the Forrester Research Survey 2008 of 600 North American business executives at companies with $1 billion or more in revenue as summarized in "The State of the CIO' 09: The Survey" *CIO* (January 1, 2009): 54.

2. The figure of 35 percent is quoted in Matt Marshall, "Aggregate Knowledge Raises $5M from Kleiner, on a Roll"

www.venturebeat.com. (December 10, 2006). Although there was some apparent dispute about the figure, Greg Linden, a driving force behind Amazon's personalization capabilities, endorsed the figure as likely accurate on the basis of his earlier experiences at Amazon. See *glinden.blogspot.com* (December 11, 2006).

3. Erik Brynjolfsson, and Michael Schrage, "The New, Faster Face of Innovation" *MIT Sloan Management Review,* http: sloanreview.mit.edu/business-insight (August 17, 2009).

Selected Bibliography

Altshuller, Genrich. *The Innovation Algorithm: TRIZ, Systematic Innovation and Technical Creativity.* Worcester, MA: Technical Innovation Center, Inc., 1999.

Argyris, Chris, and Donald A. Schon. *Organizational Learning.* New York: Addison-Wesley, 1978.

Barabasi, Albert-Laszlo. *Linked: The New Science of Networks.* Cambridge, MA: Perseus Publishing, 2002.

——. "Scale-Free Networks: A Decade and Beyond." *Science* 325 (July 24, 2009): 412–413.

Behrens, Timothy, Laurence Hunt, and Mathew Rushworth. "The Computation of Social Behavior." *Science* 324 (May 29, 2009): 1160–1164.

Besanko, David, David Dranove, and Mark Shanley. *Economics of Strategy.* New York: John Wiley and Sons, 1996.

Bryan, Lowell L., and Claudia I. Joyce. *Mobilizing Minds: Creating Wealth from Talent in the 21st-Century Organization.* New York: McGraw-Hill, 2007.

Butts, Carter T. "Revisiting the Foundations of Network Analysis." *Science* 325 (July 24, 2009): 414–416.

Carr, Nicholas G. *Does IT Matter?: Information Technology and the Corrosion of Competitive Advantage.* Boston: Harvard Business School Publishing, 2004.

Chesbrough, Henry. *Open Innovation: The New Imperative for Creating and Profiting from Technology.* Boston: Harvard Business School Press, 2003.

Christensen, Clayton M. *The Innovator's Dilemma: When New Technologies Cause Great Firms to Fail.* Boston: Harvard Business School Press, 1997.

Davenport, Thomas H., and Laurence Prusak. *Working Knowledge: How Organizations Manage What They Know.* Boston: Harvard Business School Press, 1998.

De Geus, Arie. *The Living Company.* Boston: Harvard Business School Press, 1997.

Dixit, Avinash K., and Robert S. Pindyck. *Investment under Uncertainty.* Princeton: Princeton University Press, 1994.

Dunbar, Robin. *Grooming, Gossip, and the Evolution of Language.* Cambridge, MA: Harvard University Press, 1998.

Fair, Damien, et al. "Functional Brain Networks Develop From a 'Local to Distributed' Organization." *PLOS Computational Biology* 5, no. 5 (May 2009): 1–14.

Flinn, Steven, and Naomi Moneypenny. "Adaptive Recombinant Systems." *World International Property Organization* publication no. WO/2005/054982 (June 16, 2005).

——. "Generative Investment Process." *World International Property Organization* publication no. WO/2005/103983 (November 3, 2005).

——. "Adaptive Recombinant Processes." *World International Property Organization* publication no. WO/2005/116852 (December 8, 2005).

Garvin, David A. *Learning in Action: A Guide to Putting the Learning Organization to Work.* Boston: Harvard Business School Press, 2000.

Haeckel, Stephan H. *Adaptive Enterprise: Creating and Leading Sense-and-Respond Organizations.* Boston: Harvard Business School Press, 1999.

Hagel III, John, John Seely Brown, and Lang Davison. "The Big Shift: Measuring the Forces of Change." *Harvard Business Review* (July-August 2009): 86–89.

Hagel III, John, and Marc Singer. "Unbundling the Corporation." *Harvard Business Review* (March-April 1999): 133–141.

Halevy, Alon, Peter Norvig, and Fernando Pereira. "The Unreasonable Effectiveness of Data." *IEEE Intelligent Systems* (March/April 2009): 8–12.

Hammer, Michael, and James Champy. *Reengineering the Corporation: A Manifesto for Business Revolution.* New York: HarperCollins, 1993.

Hargadon, Andrew. *How Breakthroughs Happen: The Surprising Truth about How Companies Innovate.* Boston: Harvard Business School Publishing, 2003.

Hargadon, Andrew, and Robert Sutton. "Building an Innovation Factory." *Harvard Business Review* (May-June 2000): 157–166.

Hawkins, Jeff, and Sandra Blakeslee. *On Intelligence*. New York: Times Books, 2004.

Hertz, John, Anders Krogh, and Richard G. Palmer. *Introduction to the Theory of Neural Computation*. Redwood City, CA: Addison-Wesley, 1991.

Howard, Ronald A. *The Foundations of Decision Analysis*. Stanford University Manuscript in Progress, 1998.

Kiani, Roozbeh, and Michael Shadlen. "Representation of Confidence Associated with a Decision by Neurons in the Parietal Cortex." *Science* 324 (May 8, 2009): 759–764.

Klir, George J. *Uncertainty and Information: Foundations of Generalized Information Theory*. Hoboken, NJ: John Wiley and Sons, 2006.

Kosko, Bart. *Fuzzy Thinking: The New Science of Fuzzy Logic*. New York: Hyperion, 1993.

MacKay, David J. C. *Information Theory, Inference, and Learning Algorithms*. Cambridge, UK: Cambridge University Press, 2003.

Meltzoff, Andrew N., et al. "Foundations for a New Science of Learning." *Science* 325 (July 17, 2009): 284–288.

Minsky, Marvin. *The Society of Mind*. New York: Simon and Schuster, 1985.

Pedrycz, Witold, and Fernando Gomide. *An Introduction to Fuzzy Sets: Analysis and Design*. Cambridge, MA: The MIT Press, 1998.

Pinker, Steven. *The Language Instinct*. New York: HarperCollins, 1995.

Porter, Michael E. *Competitive Strategy: Techniques for Analyzing Industries and Competitors*. New York: The Free Press, 1980.

—— *Competitive Advantage: Creating and Sustaining Superior Performance*. New York: The Free Press, 1985.

Rummler, Geary A., and Alan P. Brache. *Improving Performance: How to Manage the White Space on the Organization Chart*. San Francisco: Jossey-Bass, 1990.

Schrage, Michael. *Serious Play: How the World's Best Companies Simulate to Innovate*. Boston: Harvard Business School Publishing, 2000.

Senge, Peter M. *The Fifth Discipline: The Art & Practice of the Learning Organization*. New York: Random House, 1992.

Shirky, Clay. "Gin, Television, and Social Surplus." *www.shirky.com* (April 26, 2008).

Slywotzky, Adrian J., and David J. Morrison. *The Profit Zone: How Strategic Business Design Will Lead You to Tomorrow's Profits.* New York: Random House, 1997.

Spitzer, Manfred. *The Mind within the Net: Models of Learning, Thinking, and Acting.* Cambridge, MA: The MIT Press, 1999.

Surowiecki, James. *The Wisdom of Crowds: Why the Many Are Smarter Than the Few and How Collective Wisdom Shapes Business, Economies, Societies and Nations.* New York: Doubleday, 2004.

Sutton, Robert I. *Weird Ideas That Work: 11 1/2 Practices for Promoting, Managing, and Sustaining Innovation.* New York: The Free Press, 2001.

Strogatz, Steven. *Sync: The Emerging Science of Spontaneous Order.* New York: Hyperion, 2003.

Thomke, Stefan H. *Experimentation Matters: Unlocking the Potential of New Technologies for Innovation.* Boston: Harvard Business School Publishing, 2003.

Treacy, Michael, and Fred Wiersema. *The Discipline of Market Leaders: Choose Your Customers, Narrow Your Focus, Dominate Your Market.* Reading, MA: Addison-Wesley, 1995.

Vapnik, Vladimir N. *The Nature of Statistical Learning Theory.* New York: Springer-Verlag, 2000.

Wasserman, Stanley, and Katherine Faust. *Social Network Analysis: Methods and Applications.* Cambridge, UK. Cambridge University Press, 1994.

Watts, Duncan J. *Six Degrees: The Science of a Connected Age.* New York: W. W. Norton and Company, 2003.

Wolfram, Stephen. *A New Kind of Science.* Champaign, IL: Wolfram Media, 2002.

Index